The Behavior Code
Companion

The Behavior Code Companion

Strategies, Tools, and Interventions for Supporting Students with Anxiety-Related or Oppositional Behaviors

JESSICA MINAHAN

Harvard Education Press
Cambridge, Massachusetts

Fourth Printing, 2016
Copyright © 2014 by the President and Fellows of Harvard College

Library of Congress Control Number 2014940447

Paperback ISBN 978-1-61250-751-4
Library Edition 978-1-61250-752-1

Published by Harvard Education Press,
an imprint of the Harvard Education Publishing Group

Harvard Education Press
8 Story Street
Cambridge, MA 02138

Cover Design: Wilcox Design
Cover Photo: © Jaime Monfort/Moment/Getty Images
The typefaces used in this book are Minion and Myriad Pro.

Contents

Introduction

Mental health challenges are prevalent among school-aged children in this country. An estimated 21 percent of American teenagers have struggled with a serious and debilitating mental health problem at some point during their school-age years.[1]

It should come as no surprise that overburdened teachers are overwhelmed with the change in the makeup of a given classroom today—the rates of students with mental health challenges, including anxiety disorders, attention deficit/hyperactivity disorder (ADHD), depression, and autism, is on the rise. In a classroom of twenty-four students, roughly one-third may suffer from anxiety-related and other challenging behaviors.

Heroic teachers are facing this challenge with little to no training in mental health and behavioral principles. School systems—while identifying social-emotional learning as a need—are prioritizing other competing initiatives for professional development, leaving teachers to learn on the job and rely on their instincts. In this environment, students with mental health issues or challenging behavior remain at risk for poor outcomes such as disconnectedness from school, academic failure, poor social adjustment, and a disproportionate amount of suspensions and detentions.

The problem is compounded when we take a behavioral approach that disregards a student's mental health disorder: for example, a student with distractibility from a history of trauma may be seen as simply avoiding schoolwork, or mood swings from a student with a diagnosed mood disorder may be seen as only a method of seeking attention. Misinterpretations like these do not always lead to effective interventions.

Teachers should not be expected to be therapists; nor should they be expected to understand effectively and teach students with mental health disorders or with challenging behavior without proper training. However, intervening successfully with these students requires a shift in how we typically understand behavior and in our traditional behavioral strategies—a shift that requires education and practice. Teachers need a new approach to understanding behavior as well as a toolbox of strategies that allows them to intervene successfully within the context of sustained, cohesive support involving school mental health professionals, administrators, parents, and community agencies.

RESPONSE TO *THE BEHAVIOR CODE*

The Behavior Code: A Practical Guide to Understanding and Teaching the Most Challenging Students, written with Nancy Rappaport, associate professor of psychiatry at Harvard Medical School, and published by the Harvard Education Press in 2012, was the first book to provide this type of information on practical interventions for teachers. The approach combines a deep understanding of the psychological profiles of students with the most challenging behaviors and evidence-based behavioral strategies to produce an intervention plan that can be easily implemented in schools. *The Behavior Code* details how to develop this type of plan, called a FAIR Behavior Intervention Plan, for students with the most challenging profiles in school—students with oppositional, withdrawn, sexualized, and anxiety-related behaviors. The acronym FAIR stands for the four components of a behavior intervention plan: functional hypothesis, accommodations, interaction strategies, and response strategies.

The Behavior Code asks teachers and school professionals to shift away from behavior programs that emphasize rewards and consequences of behavior to a program that focuses on building the skills students need to exhibit appropriate behavior. The book also encourages educators to adopt a preventative approach that allows them to be proactive and less reactive to students with challenging behavior by using informed accommodations and by rethinking their interactions with these students.

The feedback to this new approach has been overwhelmingly positive. People are thrilled to see that with the FAIR Behavior Intervention Plan, students who have been struggling for years are making progress. Educators have been inspired to shift their thinking and impart their new view to colleagues and parents.

Since the publication of *The Behavior Code*, however, I have received many requests for more information on effective interventions for two of the four types of students with challenging behaviors covered by the book: anxiety-related and oppositional behaviors. Considering the feedback from teachers, psychologists, special educators, school leaders, and parents, there is a crucial demand for additional guidance in delivering interventions and creating and implementing FAIR Behavior Intervention Plans for these students.

In workshops and seminars, and in working as a consultant to districts across the country, I have also had a chance to see which interventions have proved most difficult for educators to implement and where the sticking points most often occur. Educators have told me that some concepts critical to working successfully with students exhibiting anxiety-related and/or oppositional behaviors—such as cognitive shifts and skills required for transitions from one activity to another—do not come as easily as others.

I have written *The Behavior Code Companion* to respond to teachers' most prevalent concerns around supporting students K–6 with anxiety-related and oppositional behavior. In light of my sixteen years of experience consulting to teachers struggling to support students with mental health challenges, I believe this guide provides the needed guidance and help with troubleshooting from someone who has been in schools and has had to problem solve real-life practical solutions to complex situations. My primary goals in writing this guide are to help teachers with the following shifts in their teaching practice:

- Learn new tools that can be put to use immediately in the classroom.
- Provide themselves with an adequate opportunity to reflect on and practice new strategies.
- Gain confidence in implementing interventions they may be struggling with.
- Determine whether a chosen intervention for a student is actually effective.

Also, while *The Behavior Code* endeavored to cover the widest possible range of situations within the scope of the book, some issues weren't discussed in depth or were omitted entirely. *The Behavior Code Companion* will provide additional interventions that were not included in *The Behavior Code*, among them, ways to assess student progress, mitigate the effects of a student's anxious thinking, engage students in learning which interventions work for them, assess correct implementation of interventions, and how use of the protocols keeps a student safe in a crisis.

HOW TO USE THIS GUIDE

The Behavior Code Companion was written to be used in conjunction with *The Behavior Code*. Each chapter of this guide begins with a review of important concepts from the original book, along with extended information, new strategies and interventions, and guidance on how to implement important interventions for students with anxiety-related or oppositional behaviors. The chapters also include implementation tips and stories of successful interventions, titled "Tales from the Field." To protect the students' privacy, I have changed their names and some details of the particular situations in the book.

Each chapter contains reflection and other exercises as well as case studies designed to help the reader understand and practice the functional analysis (F), accommodations (A), interaction strategies (I), and response strategies (R) that are at the heart of the FAIR Behavior Intervention Plan. Chapters 1 through 3 address concepts and interventions that can apply to both types of students addressed in this guide, while chapters 4 and 5 contain information particular to each type in turn. Suggested answers to some of the reflection, practice, and case study exercises are offered in the appendix section to support educators who may be using this guide outside of a formal training session.

This guide was written to build skills and capacity so that educators feel empowered to create effective FAIR Behavior Intervention Plans. Chapter 6, therefore, offers extended opportunities to practice using information from both books to analyze traditional classroom behavior plans and create new FAIR Behavior Intervention Plans for students.

Chapter 7 introduces new types of data sheets and checklists intended to help teachers judge whether an intervention or FAIR Behavior Intervention Plan is working and whether they are implementing the interventions consistently and correctly. One of the keys to effective interventions is not simply to make an intervention plan that is based on data, but also to use data to analyze whether the students (and educators) are benefiting from the plan. Only in this way can we as educators say that we are doing our best to help these students develop the skills they need to experience success in school—and in life.

In appendix A, you will find language and advice on including FAIR Behavior Intervention Plan accommodations and interventions in IEPs (individualized education programs). Protocols for common crisis situations such as safety (aggression) and a student's bolting from the classroom or building, making a threat, and making a self-harm statements are provided in appendix B so that teams can tailor these well-informed plans to the needs of their students and ensure the safety of the students, the students' peers, and all involved school personnel.

In my work with schools, I have been impressed by the growing number of digital tools and apps that have proved incredibly helpful in working with students with challenging behavior. Therefore, I have included suggestions for using technology throughout the chapters and in a special resource section on apps in appendix C.

Blank updated FAIR Behavior Intervention Plans, and FAIR Behavior Intervention Plans tailored for students with anxiety and oppositional behavior, are also included in appendixes D, E, and F for easy use.

This guide is intended to be used by any individual looking for guidance alone or with members of a student's team. (For students receiving special education services, *the team* refers to the IEP team; for students not receiving special education services, the school team typically includes the teacher, a mental health professional, and an administrator.)

Whenever possible, engaging as a team in the activities described in this companion book will help schools make decisions about interventions and which members of the team have which roles in supporting students (e.g., who is going to do the explicit teaching and who will run an alternative lunch group). Building capacity in the adults this way will help many students exhibiting challenging behavior in the future.

A final note on terminology. As in *The Behavior Code*, much of this guide is addressed to teachers, but it can be useful to anyone supporting students in the classroom. My intended audience includes school psychologists, social workers, guidance and adjustment counselors (referred to as mental health professionals in this guide), general education teachers in inclusive settings, special education teachers in self-contained classrooms, educational and clinical specialists and administrators, inclusion aides, classroom assistants, and interns. Parents who found *The Behavior Code* helpful as part of the student's team and applied its practical suggestions at home will find *The Behavior Code Companion* an additional go-to resource.

Certainly, students with mental health challenges are currently struggling in schools, and teachers and school teams are trying to muster the strength to sustain their effort despite continual setbacks and heartbreaks. But there is reason for optimism. By cracking the behavior code, we can continue to transform our understanding of behavior—by empowering students with skills and adaptive ways to cope.

I am thrilled to offer this guide for teachers and all those who found *The Behavior Code* to be a beacon of hope and a new way forward using effective solutions to seemingly intractable behaviors. With the additional tools and insights in this guide, I believe that teachers can become less overwhelmed by a student's psychiatric diagnosis or life situation, feel more comfortable in unexpected moments, and gain confidence with each small success. Students can learn to take a deep breath instead of yelling, monitor themselves during an assembly, and independently initiate work. Building capacity in school-based teams while fortifying skills within the student is a start toward real and sustained progress.

CHAPTER 1

Cracking the Code

Embracing a New Perspective on Behavior

In this chapter, we will practice embracing six essential concepts that help us understand, productively intervene with, and support students with challenging behavior. We will also reflect on assumptions that may interfere with the adoption of these concepts and discuss how to monitor your emotions when you are faced with a student exhibiting challenging behavior so that you can be optimally productive and consistent.

SIX ESSENTIAL CONCEPTS OF BEHAVIOR REVIEW

Understanding the following critical concepts helps teachers choose how to intervene better with students' problematic behavior:

- *Misbehavior is a symptom of an underlying cause.* A student would behave if he could—some students can't behave optimally. If the student is displaying problematic, maladaptive behavior, it is a symptom of an underdeveloped skill.
- *Behavior is communication.* Even though students' behavior can look bizarre or disruptive, their actions are purposeful and represent the student's attempt to solve a problem.
- *Behavior has a function.* Mark Durand categorizes all human behaviors as being motivated by four functions: to get attention, to escape or avoid something, to

gain something tangible like an object or an agenda, or to gain sensory (smell, taste, feel) satisfaction.[1]

- *Behavior occurs in patterns.* Behavior does not "come out of nowhere"; there is a reason, and typically, there is a pattern.
- *The only behavior teachers can control is their own.* Good behavior plans, such as the FAIR Behavior Intervention Plan, are really a guide for helping teachers develop new behaviors to interact with challenging students in a more productive and preemptive way.
- *Behavior can be changed.* To change inappropriate behavior, students need to be taught new ways to behave, rather than just managing the behavior in the short term.

SIX ESSENTIAL CONCEPTS OF BEHAVIOR EXPANDED

Students with anxiety-related and oppositional behavior can be extremely challenging in schools. When a student is disrespectful, rude, oppositional, or disruptive, it evokes little sympathy in many adults and often creates stress for the adult. The behavior often looks purposeful, and a disrespectful comment may also have a humiliating or demoralizing effect on the teacher if it occurs in front of an audience, which can hurt her relationship with the student.

To accepting the six essential concepts about behavior, you need a bit of a leap of faith. Students' challenging behavior looks purposeful and premeditated; it seems to be totally in the students' control and an entrenched part of their personality. However, these behaviors are largely counterintuitive and not easily understood. Our automatic responses to these behaviors are often counterproductive, and our instinct is often to punish.

Only by changing how we think about behavior can we effectively reach these students. When teachers think differently about behavior, they can redirect their efforts to discovering and teaching the underdeveloped skills that are often the cause of inappropriate behavior. Shifting our thinking about behavior in this way will lead to productive planning for the student as described in the rest of this guide and is the first step toward the student's long-term behavior change. The best way to develop and internalize these concepts is through practice, which allows our instinctive response to challenging behavior to be a more productive, consistent, and effective one.

> ### Tales from the Field
>
> Several years ago, when I was an inclusion/behavior specialist in an urban, low-performing K–8 school, I carried a pager with me. When there was a behavior incident, I would be paged, and the only information I received was the room number. I would quickly walk toward the room, not knowing what I was going to walk into (possibilities included a student with a weapon, a student running out of the school, or a student engaged in self-harming behavior). I learned to recite these six essential concepts to myself on the way so that when I entered the room, they would guide me to think productively and (most importantly) avoid unproductive assumptions, such as thinking that the student was acting out on purpose or that the disruptive behavior couldn't possibly change, given the student's dysfunctional home life.

Monitoring Our Emotions

Certain student behaviors, such as disrespectful comments, verbal aggression, swearing, and unkind remarks or actions, can produce an emotional reaction in teachers. It is human nature for us to have negative reactions to some of these behaviors, because of our own histories, personal experiences, or tolerance levels. The more we are aware of our own perspective, triggers, and tolerance, the better we can be at managing ourselves when faced with a behavior incident. Developing a plan for situations that we know may be particularly challenging to us (e.g., switching off with another teacher when a student insults you) can help us react as effectively as possible.

> ### Tales from the Field
>
> Hannah, a fifth-grade student with poor social skills and anxiety, commented on Mr. Petrov's spelling one day in class: "You spelled that wrong! Although it's not a surprise, since you only went to *community college*."

> Mr. Petrov relayed this incident to me with a shaky voice and red face: "No other occupation would ask me to endure public humiliation." He told me he had removed himself from the student immediately after the comment (by walking over to a small group of students in the back of the room). I told him this was a smart response and helped him brainstorm some other strategies to help him stay calm and intervene effectively, if a similar situation arose in the future.

Sustaining Effort

Working with students with challenging behavior can require a great deal of energy, and teachers often experience stress, frustration, and feelings of inadequacy. It is important to take care of yourself while you are supporting your students. Please review chapter 7 of *The Behavior Code* for ideas on supporting your own well-being and sustaining effort throughout the school year. The same chapter also provides ideas for how administrators can best support teachers who are working tirelessly with students with challenging behavior.

REFLECT

How Do You Think About Behavior?

Take this quick assessment and see which essential behavior concepts you have already adopted. Read each statement, and circle the correct answer or answers. Which behavior concepts do you need to practice or want to think about some more? How will you practice?

1. I believe misbehavior is due to an underdeveloped skill.

   Never   Seldom   Sometimes   Often   Always

2. I remember that behavior is one way a student communicates, and I try to decipher the communicative meaning.

   Never   Seldom   Sometimes   Often   Always

3. I remember that there is a function to the student's behavior, and I take ABC (antecedent, behavior, consequence) data to hypothesize this.

   Never   Seldom   Sometimes   Often   Always

4. I understand that behavior typically occurs in patterns.

Never   Seldom   Sometimes   Often   Always

5. I believe that the only behavior I have control over is my own and that by changing my interactions, it can contribute to a more desired response from the student.

Never   Seldom   Sometimes   Often   Always

6. I believe that behavior can be changed, even with students who demonstrate extremely challenging behaviors.

Never   Seldom   Sometimes   Often   Always

Setting Aside Our Assumptions

We all make assumptions. In school, our assumptions are based on our prior knowledge about behavior and students. For the most part, these assumptions are helpful and serve us well (e.g., when a student is lurking near the teacher's desk, we assume she wants help). For the students we are focusing on in this book, however, we have to set aside our assumptions and think about behavior differently, in a way that may not be intuitive. But before we set them aside, it is important to examine our assumptions and beliefs in order to understand how they may compete with the new way of looking at behavior.

The following are some common assumptions about behavior that, in my experience, may not be helpful in understanding students with anxiety-related or oppositional behavior:

- Behavior is purposeful.
- He *should* be able to do it.
- He will become reliant on help if I accommodate him.
- It's not anything I'm doing.
- Doing *X* (e.g., using language, participating in class, waiting) is easy to accomplish.
- She can easily do *X* instead.
- It's not fair to the other kids.
- This is sending a poor message to the other students.
- We shouldn't allow a kid to get away with it and not punish her.

Examining Your Assumptions

Read the statements about students' behavior in the left column and the hidden assumptions that these statements imply on the right. The assumptions are not necessarily right or wrong but guide the teacher's intervention so it is important to be aware of. Then answer the questions below.

Statement about behavior	Hidden assumptions
"If he needs a break, he can lift his head off the desk, raise his hand, and ask for one."	• Raising his hand and waiting for a teacher to call on him is as easy as putting his head down. • Asking publicly for a break is easy and nonthreatening. • The student has the ability to use language when upset.
"She is going to middle school next year, so she needs to organize her own folder, and I am no longer going to help."	• Pulling away support allows a student to practice a skill, and this will improve the skill. • Telling a student she is old enough and should be able to do it will lead to the student's showing this ability.
"Well, he finished his math sheet yesterday, so he is obviously choosing not to do it today. He was lazy, so I will send his unfinished work home for homework."	• He is behaving that way on purpose, and it is in the student's control. • Giving him more homework will teach him to do his work in school.
"She can turn her behavior on and off."	• She is behaving that way on purpose—it is in her control.
"He needs to practice being in the cafeteria at least once per week."	• Anxiety and poor behavior performance is due to lack of practice. • The student doesn't require support. • Being in a stressful environment enables the student to tolerate the environment rather than cause more anxiety and aversion.
"She doesn't need a break. She just had PE."	• Physical education class was a pleasant, regulating experience. • Any movement is helpful and should be considered a break. • The skills required to successfully participate in physical education (e.g., social interaction, waiting, performing in front of peers) are easy.

1. Do I have any of the above-mentioned beliefs about behavior? Which ones?

   _____

2. Has it been difficult for me to learn a new perspective on behavior for the students discussed in *The Behavior Code*? If so, why?

   _____

3. Do certain beliefs I hold about behavior and students interfere with my adoption of the essential behavior concepts?

_____

4. Are there certain student behaviors that are the most difficult for me to understand or accept because they evoke an emotional response and it's hard for me to think as productively?

_____

5. Which essential behavior principle is the hardest for me to understand or believe?

_____

CASE STUDY

Julian, a Student with Anxiety

Let's practice using the six essential concepts as a lens for viewing behavior in a different way. Read the following case study, and review the interpretation of the essential concepts in exhibit 1.1.

Julian is a second grade-student with anxiety. When meeting with his mother at parent-teacher conferences, Julian's teacher describes Julian's behavior over the past week as follows:

> Julian has gone from doing little work to refusing to do almost anything. When asked to do work or when given the suggestion he might want to start, he says, "I am not doing it," and "That's not happening." He spent two hours asleep in the corner of the classroom on Wednesday, and on Thursday he was pacing around the student's desks and sitting on the radiator in the back of the room whenever he was asked to do work. Prior to this week, the teacher was able to get him to do some reading and science work, but he refused to attempt any math or writing work all year thus far.
>
> Julian had an incident last week with a peer during kickball at recess and has since refused to go to recess. Instead, he has been sitting in the classroom, typically humming and looking at the fish tank as the teacher tries to cajole him to go outside.

EXHIBIT 1.1   **Six essential behavior concepts for Julian**

Here are some possible ways to reframe an understanding of Julian's behavior.

Essential concept of behavior	*Possibilities or questions to investigate*
Misbehavior is a symptom of an underlying cause.	Underdeveloped skills may include: • Self-regulation • Self-calming • Flexible thinking • Transition skills • Writing skills • Thought stopping • Social skills (i.e., perspective taking) • Executive functioning (if needed) • Self-monitoring • Initiating a task
Behavior is communication.	Avoidance behavior may mean Julian is trying to communicate: • I need help. • I am nervous. • I think I can't do it. • I've had a bad experience doing something similar. • I don't know where to start. • I don't feel safe taking the risk. • I need to calm down, or regulate. • Inconsistent behavior patterns may mean Julian is trying to communicate: • I am anxious. • I didn't catch myself early enough, and I can't handle anything right now. • I need help to calm down, or regulate.
Behavior has a function.	Julian is motivated by escape or avoidance and can also be motivated by attention (as evidenced by his walking around peers' desks).

Essential concept of behavior	Possibilities or questions to investigate
Behavior occurs in patterns.	There are some consistent patterns of avoidance behavior (consistent activities he is trying to avoid)—difficult situations or activities include: <ul><li>Unstructured times</li><li>Transitions</li><li>Social demands</li><li>Novel events or unexpected change</li><li>Exposure to an academic subject that the student has weakness in</li><li>There are also inconsistent patterns, which can seem random, due to:</li><li>Internal thoughts</li><li>Subtle environmental triggers</li><li>Level of regulation (e.g., anxiety was building throughout the day)</li></ul>
The only behavior teachers can control is their own.	The teacher can learn to respond to Julian's challenging behavior in a different way (e.g., not reprimanding him—not giving attention—when he is pacing around the room). And the teacher can give directions to work in a way that is more likely to promote compliance.
Behavior can be changed.	School staff can learn to teach Julian underdeveloped skills; teach more appropriate replacement strategies; and accommodate the environment, curriculum, and the way they interact with him so he no longer needs to engage in inappropriate behavior.
	Julian can learn to catch himself early and self-regulate—preventing anxiety from leading to behavior or academic challenges.

CASE STUDY

Malik, a Student with Anxiety

Now read the case study below, and practice being curious about Malik's behavior. Brainstorm the information you can extrapolate from his behavior over the past week, and answer the questions in the second column in exhibit 1.2.

Malik is a fifth-grade student. His teacher calls a meeting with the principal and school psychologist out of concern. The teacher describes Malik's behavior over the past week as follows:

Malik is getting very little work completed in English this week. He refused to do a social studies assignment where he needs to write about a country of his choosing, but asked for an extra-credit assignment in science. He had a great day Tuesday (he got work done except for English class and was complying with requests), and then on Wednesday and Thursday, he refused to come in from the recess yard twice. The second time, the school psychologist had to go out and coax him inside, which took fifteen minutes.

EXHIBIT 1.2   **Six essential behavior concepts for Malik**

Essential behavior concept	Information to extrapolate from student's behavior
Misbehavior is a symptom of an underlying cause.	What skills might Malik need to develop?
Behavior is communication.	What might Malik be communicating through his behavior?
Behavior has a function.	What do you hypothesize is the function of Malik's behavior?
Behavior occurs in patterns.	What patterns do you see in Malik's behavior? What are some antecedents that lead to Malik's anxiety and subsequent challenging behavior?
The only behavior teachers have control over is their own.	What are some ways the teacher can initiate interactions and respond to Malik's behavior to help him demonstrate appropriate behavior?
Behavior can be changed.	What is the behavior goal for Malik?

Reframing Our Understanding of Behavior

Now put yourself in the role of a consultant working with a teacher who has not learned about the six essential concepts of behavior. How would you help this adult reframe their view of the following specific behavior incident? (Possible answers are provided in appendix G.)

Scenario: Joe pushes Keiko off the swing and then gets on it himself.

Teacher's response: "Joe is being mean! He's spoiled and thinks the world revolves around him!"

How might you respond to this adult by reframing the student's behavior using each of the essential concepts? Write how you would respond to the adult under each essential concept listed. What would you say to him or her using that concept?

Misbehavior is a symptom of an underlying cause.

Behavior is communication.

Behavior has a function.

Behavior occurs in patterns.

The only behavior teachers can control is their own.

Behavior can be changed.

CHAPTER 2

The FAIR
Behavior Intervention Plan

Practicing the Fundamentals

Now that you have internalized the six essential concepts of behavior, we will practice using them to shape the behavior of our most challenging students. In *The Behavior Code*, we introduced a new type of behavior intervention plan called the FAIR Behavior Intervention Plan. As explained earlier, the acronym represents the four parts of a successful intervention plan for student behavior: a functional hypothesis about the intent or function of the student's behavior, the accommodations necessary to help the student function better, interaction strategies to promote the desired behavior, and optimal response strategies should an intervention step fail. In this chapter, we will practice with the building blocks needed to construct a FAIR Behavior Intervention Plan: collecting and analyzing ABC (antecedent, behavior, and consequences) data and writing clear target behavior definitions.

But first, there is an intermediate, often overlooked step to changing a student's behavior. Students can find replacement behaviors that fulfill the function of the inappropriate behavior—but in an appropriate way. Teaching students to stop communicating through inappropriate behavior and to communicate in a more functional and expected way (called *functional communication*) is a common replacement behavior to teach. Choosing which replacement behavior to teach a student is difficult, so this chapter allows for adequate practice and reflection.

REPLACEMENT BEHAVIOR: REVIEW

Teaching replacement behaviors is an essential part of the *A*—or accommodations component—in a FAIR Behavior Intervention Plan. A replacement behavior is an appropriate behavior that serves the same function as an inappropriate behavior, allowing students to meet their needs while they build the necessary skills for behaving appropriately without accommodations. For example, instead of disrespectfully refusing to read out loud during reading group, students can learn to ask to read quietly, perhaps by holding up a card that says "I pass"—a behavior that gets them what they want in an appropriate way. The replacement behavior must get the same desired outcome, be just as efficient, and be within the student's ability.

REPLACEMENT BEHAVIOR: EXPANDED

A replacement behavior should be at least *as* efficient as the undesired behavior, but it will be accepted and learned more quickly by the student if it is *more* efficient.

Tales from the Field

I was called in to consult on a sixth-grade student, Sean, who was announcing he needed to see the nurse and leaving to go to her office several times per week during class. The teacher understood this as a way of avoiding a difficult task, but chose a replacement behavior that was more difficult than the problem behavior. She asked Sean to raise his hand, wait to be called on, and request an out-of-class break instead. Asking to go to the nurse without waiting to be called on was faster, required less language, and didn't publicly acknowledge that he needed a break. The teacher and I decided to have Sean get up, walk to the door, grab a break pass off the designated hook, and take his out-of-class break. I spoke to Sean about the plan, and he liked it, especially because the other kids "didn't have to know his business." He easily learned this replacement behavior, as it was easier (requiring no talking, no waiting, and no public acknowledgment that he needed to leave) than the original behavior.

Tip It can be difficult to understand why it is a good idea to give a student a way to escape from demands, as our instinct is often not to let students avoid a situation. But teaching a replacement behavior, the first small step in behavior change, is crucial: getting needs met through appropriate means, rather than inappropriate ones. This step is not giving in to the student; it is shaping inappropriate escape motivated behavior to a more appropriate one.

Social Validity

Before choosing a replacement behavior to teach your student, make sure it's socially valid.[1] Social validity means that the replacement behaviors are acceptable to both the student and the teacher implementing them. For example, it's important to make sure the students don't think the strategy makes them stand out and that the teacher doesn't think the strategy is too difficult to implement.

Functional Communication

One of the most effective and universally applicable replacement behaviors to teach is functional communication. Through this preventative intervention, a student learns an appropriate communicative behavior as a replacement to an inappropriate one.[2]

Once the function of an inappropriate behavior is hypothesized through ABC data or a functional behavior assessment (FBA), a socially acceptable communicative response that achieves the same results should be chosen and then used across all teachers and staff.[3] Other criteria for replacement behaviors (i.e., get the same desired response, be just as efficient, and be within the student's ability) need to be addressed, but the first step is hypothesizing the function of the original behavior (we cannot decipher the function without an FBA). See table 2.1 for examples of functional communication for attention- and escape-motivated behaviors. Notice that the hypothesized function is equivalent for all functional communication responses.

Tip Be sure not to make the replacement behaviors too long or complicated. They need to be efficient ways of attaining the desired result. Functional communication can also be nonverbal, such as pointing to a picture or signaling with a nonverbal sign (e.g., the American Sign Language sign for break).

TABLE 2.1   **Examples of functional communication**

Behavior	Consequence	Hypothesized function of behavior	Functional communication	Consequence	Hypothesized function of behavior
Making a silly comment to the teacher	Teacher responds by repeatedly telling student to stop	Attention	"Am I doing a good job?"	Teacher answers the student	Attention
Yelling, "I can't do this!"	Teacher offers the student help	Attention	"Can you help me?"	Teacher offers help	Attention
Saying, "This is stupid. I'm not doing it"	Student keeps head on the desk until the end of class	Escape	"Can I have a break?"	Student is allowed to stop working and take a break	Escape
Asking to get a drink of water	Student walks to get a drink and returns six minutes later	Escape	Holding up a break card	Student is allowed to stop working and take a break	Escape

Tip   Whenever possible, have the student be involved in choosing functional communication or any replacement behavior. The student may have reasons for preferring certain strategies to others that you would not have guessed (e.g., "I would never say, 'Am I doing a good job?' but I'll say, 'Can I speak to you?'"). Agreement with the student also helps with buy-in and social validity.

Functional Communication

Alone or with team members, fill in the hypothesized function of the behavior, a functional communication replacement, the predicted consequence of the teacher, and the hypothesized function of the functional communication. Make sure the functions match as well.

Behavior	Consequence	Hypothesized function of behavior	Functional communication replacement	Consequence	Hypothesized function of behavior
Tevan interrupts the teacher when she is talking to another adult	Teacher stops talking to the adult and reminds him to wait until she finishes her conversation				
Jill yells at the teacher, "You're ignoring me!"	Teacher tells her she will help her in a few minutes				
When she is upset, Carla walks out of class to see the social worker	Teacher asks Carla to raise her hand and wait to be called on, and then the student will be able to go				
During snack, John announces to peers that he has just been drafted by a professional basketball team	Teacher talks to him one on one about lying				

PRACTICE

Replacement Behavior

Now that you've practiced hypothesizing the function of the original behavior and matching it with the hypothesized function of the replacement behavior, read the original behaviors and the proposed replacement behaviors in the table. In the third column, write whether you think they are suitable replacement behaviors. If not, in the fourth column write a replacement behavior that would be more appropriate. Remember, functional communication is a replacement behavior, so using that intervention is appropriate here as well.

Guidelines for Replacement Behaviors

- The replacement behavior must *achieve the same results* as the inappropriate behavior (e.g., function: escape from a demand).
- The replacement behavior should be *as efficient as, or more efficient than,* the inappropriate behavior in getting the desired outcome.
- The replacement behavior needs to be *within the student's ability.*
- The replacement behavior must be socially valid.

Undesirable behavior	Replacement behavior	Is this an appropriate replacement behavior?	If not, what would be an appropriate replacement behavior?
Steve puts his head down when asked to read aloud during reading group	Teacher teaches him to say "I pass" instead of putting his head down		
Sue Mae draws a picture of a naked woman on her worksheet and shows a peer	Teacher teaches her to ask for help		

Undesirable behavior	Replacement behavior	Is this an appropriate replacement behavior?	If not, what would be an appropriate replacement behavior?
Julian makes burping noises during class	Teacher teaches him to only make those noises at recess		
Tim cries and bangs his fist on the desk until his teacher comes over	Teacher teaches him to put his head down quietly if he isn't going to do work		
Wen will run out of class during work periods	Teacher teaches him to ask for help when frustrated		
Jill starts crying and asks to go home during independent math work	Teacher teaches her to say, "I need help"		
Bruno has low work production during English class and often puts his head down on the desk	Teacher teaches him to write his feelings down in a notebook instead of shutting down		
Amy scribbles all over her worksheet	Teacher teaches her she needs to ask for help		

DEFINING TARGET BEHAVIOR: REVIEW

When creating a FAIR Behavior Intervention Plan, you need to start with a list that prioritizes the targeted behaviors. These behaviors should be defined and listed at the top of each FAIR Behavior Intervention Plan. Make the definition as explicit as possible to create observable, measurable definitions of the types of behaviors you are trying to track and analyze.

To do this, think about what the behavior literally looks like. Avoid words, such as *tantrum*, that could be interpreted in different ways. Instead, use a more observable description such as *screaming*, *kicking furniture*, *swiping materials off the desk*, or *stomping feet*.

DEFINING TARGET BEHAVIORS: EXPANDED

A complete definition of target behavior includes a short descriptor along with concrete examples so that any staff member collecting data or observing a student can clearly identify each behavior. The clear identification reduces miscommunication among staff and fosters common understanding and language about a student's behavior. A target behavior can be either positive (behavior to be increased) or negative (behavior to be decreased).

> ### Examples of Common Positive and Negative Target Behaviors
>
> - *Raising a hand:* Any instance in which Jimmy raises his hand and doesn't speak until he is called on before sharing information verbally in class. Example: Jimmy raises his hand and waits for the teacher to say his name before he answers the math problem. Nonexample: Jimmy raises his hand to stretch during class.
> - *Picking at fingers:* Any instance in which Tatiana manipulates the skin around her fingernail. Behaviors include pulling, scratching, digging, and ripping the skin and may or may not cause bleeding. Example: Tatiana pulls at a hangnail. Nonexample: Tatiana picks glue off her fingers after art class.

Measurable definitions, also known as operational definitions, should be measurable, observable, accurate, and complete. In addition to being clearly written so that anyone could reenact the behavior, I recommend using these four criteria to determine if a behavior definition is well written (or operational):[4]

- It is an *accurate* description of the behavior. (To evaluate this, you must have personally observed the behavior.)
- It only refers to behavioral characteristics that are *observable* by one of the five senses. No guessing or subjective judgments are required of observers.
- It is *complete*. It describes what is and is not to be considered an instance of the behavior, with at least one example and one nonexample described in terms of the observable behavior of the student.
- It is *measurable*. The behavior has at least one measurable dimension. (Possible measurable dimensions include duration, frequency, rate, latency, accuracy, permanent product, intensity, and topography or shape. See chapter 7 for an explanation of all these dimensions.)

Examples of Nonmeasurable Definitions

- *Off-task behavior:* Any time Wen is hyperactive and distracted.
- *Aggression:* Any time Fatima tries to hurt another person.

Examples of Measurable Definitions

- *Aggression:* Any instance of hitting, pushing, throwing items in another person's direction, or pinching that could result in damage to an individual. *Example*: Kai pushes his teacher's arm out of the way when she presents work materials. *Nonexample*: Kai taps peer's forearm with his index finger to get the peer's attention.
- *Environmental destruction:* Any instances of throwing items not designed to be thrown, swiping objects off surfaces, ripping paper, crumpling items, tipping over furniture, slamming doors when no people are within five feet, or hitting or kicking walls or other objects. Only count instances wherein objects are not directed toward staff or peers. *Example*: Swiping a book off the desk. *Nonexample*: Throwing a ball during physical education class (PE) or throwing away trash in the trash can. Note that directing any thrown object at a person falls under the "aggression" definition and procedure.

Positive Versus Negative Target Behaviors

It's helpful to write positive behaviors (those you want to see increased), such as replacement behaviors, as the target behaviors on the FAIR Behavior Intervention Plan. Skill building and skill improvement should be the focus of the plan. If for some reason you and your team decide to use negative behaviors (those you want to decrease), you should add positive behaviors as well.

PRACTICE

Writing Target Behaviors

Read the following definitions, and decide if they meet the criteria for an acceptable definition of a targeted behavior.

Original definition	Is it accurate?	Is it measurable?	Is it observable?	Is it complete?	What would be an operational definition?
Aggression: When Tavis is aggressive toward peers. Example: he throws a ball purposely at children.					
Teasing: When Anna teases her peers at recess or in the classroom.					

Original definition	Is it accurate?	Is it measurable?	Is it observable?	Is it complete?	What would be an operational definition?
Mouthing: Any time Tommy puts his fingers in his mouth. Nonexample: Tommy licks his finger after dripping jelly on it at lunch.					
Attention-seeking behavior: Any time Tanya wants to get her peers' attention in class.					
Impulsive behavior: Any instance of Jim's being impulsive in class.					
Aggression: Wen will hit, kick, and punch when disappointed. Example: He slaps a girl with his hand on her face after losing a game. Nonexample: He grabs a student to catch himself when he trips.					
Following directions: Any time Serita listens to the teacher or the teacher's assistant.					

ABC NOTES: ANTECEDENT, BEHAVIOR, AND CONSEQUENCE: REVIEW

Taking notes makes it easier to determine patterns of behavior and to hypothesize the function of a behavior. A simple three-column ABC format is a quick but thorough way to document behavior incidents by breaking the incident down into three parts: the *antecedent*, or what happened immediately prior to the behavior; a description of the *behavior* itself; and the *consequence*, or teacher's or peers' response immediately following the behavior.[5] ABC notes also record the setting events (those that influence behavior but are further removed in time than the antecedent).[6] Such events should be shared between the family and school as needed.

Documenting a minimum of five incidents allows us to start looking for patterns. It is important to look at the antecedents to see where the student might need support, and at the consequences to see how the responses to the behavior may have been reinforcing or maintaining it.

ABC NOTES: EXPANDED

ABC notes are not a substitute for a functional behavior assessment (FBA) or a functional analysis (FA), as they don't decipher function thoroughly and adequately, but they are an easy and effective tool for teachers to see patterns, hypothesize the function of the student's behavior, and reflect on their own responses. FBAs and FAs (assessments that decipher the function of behavior) are recommended for students with ongoing behavior issues, as multiple functions might be contributing to the students' behavior. Board-certified behavior analysts, school psychologists, special educators, or social workers trained in FBAs should conduct these more complex analyses.

Ideally, once teachers are comfortable with ABC notes, they will use the notes in conjunction with a progress-monitoring data sheet to decide whether the interventions are working and if students are making progress. Chapter 7 presents a data sheet that combines ABC and progress data and provides further explanation of different ways to collect data and assess progress. See also "Practice: Structured ABC Data Sheet" for an example of a structured ABC sheet that you might find easier and faster to use.

Taking Advantage of Technology

Data can be collected on paper or electronically. It is important to pick a data collection system you are comfortable with to ensure consistency and accuracy. See the data-collecting applications in the section "Behavior and Data Collection" in appendix C.

PRACTICE

Analyzing Stan's ABC Notes

Review Kevin's ABC data, presented in table 3.4, figure 3.1, and elsewhere in chapter 3 of *The Behavior Code*. After reading Kevin's ABC analysis in that book, read Stan's ABC analysis in exhibit 2.1 and figure 2.1 here. Do you agree with the summary of Stan's ABC notes and analysis? If not, how would you interpret Stan's behavior and its function?

EXHIBIT 2.1 **ABC notes for Stan, a kindergarten student**

Date, time, duration	Setting Events	Antecedent	Behavior	Consequences
10/6, 9:55, 6 min		Ms. Kelly tells student "recess will be indoors today—it's raining."	Stan screams and runs for Ms. Kelly and hits her in the stomach repeatedly.	Ms. Kelly physically escorts Stan into the small hallway for four minutes until he is calm.
10/6, 11:20, 1 min	Mom's boyfriend moved out of the house last night.	Ms. Kelly gives the transition warning that choice time is over: "Five more minutes, and then we switch," she says, holding her five fingers up.	Stan screams and grabs the arm of the teaching assistant to his right and motions that he is going to bite her.	Teaching assistant gets up and moves to the other side of the classroom.
10/6, 2:20, 7 min		Students are putting on their coats, and Stan is playing with a Lego in the dramatic-play area. Ms. Kelly says, "Stan, come on, it's time for the bus," and shows him the icon from his schedule.	Stan screams "No!" and ignores the demand. Ms. Kelly repeats statement, and he grabs the schedule, throws it, and then pinches his cheek and kicks the teacher.	Stan is escorted to the hallway for five minutes and then has to be escorted to the bus by two adults.

Date, time, duration	Setting Events	Antecedent	Behavior	Consequences
10/7, 9:30, 30 min	Stan reported he forgot to take his medicine in the morning	Ms. Kelly shows the class the visual schedule of literacy activities they need to accomplish. She asks them to sit at their desks to begin literacy. Stan looks at the list of activities he needs to do.	Stan yells and scratches the top of his hand, then runs for Ms. Kelly, who is holding the schedule. She blocks his first two attempts, but then he succeeds in hitting her.	Both teachers bring Stan to the hallway, where he stays for twenty-eight minutes.
10/7, 1:42, until the end of the day		Stan asks to look at the book a peer is reading. The peer tells him to wait until she's done.	Stan falls on the floor and screams. He starts pulling at his mouth. Ms. Kelly goes over to comfort him, and he continues to scream.	Stan is escorted to the nurse, and his mom is called.
10/10, 2:15		Stan gets in line to go home, but Ms. Kelly tells him to sit back at his desk because the bus won't be there for another ten minutes.	Stan pushes past the teacher and waits in the hallway for the bus.	Ms. Kelly keeps the classroom door open so that she can watch him.

FIGURE 2.1 **Analyzing Stan's ABC data**

Antecedents	Consequences
Novelty (indoor recess): /	Removed to hallway, nurse's office, or adult removes herself (indoor recess, choice time, both dismissals, literacy, peer asks for book): ℋℋ /
Transitions (choice time, dismissal, start of literacy): ///	
Asked to wait (book, dismissal): //	

ABC Summary

As we can see in figure 2.1, three incidents occurred during transitions, two occurred when Stan was asked to wait, and one incident was after an announcement that recess was being held indoors. Thus, the antecedents for Stan's behavior included transitions, his being asked to wait, and a novel change in routine.

In the consequence column, Stan successfully avoided or escaped demands.

He was removed from the class on all six occasions and subsequently avoided the task, activity, or situation. These observations show that the function of his behavior was probably escape or avoidance.

Analyzing Juanita's ABC Notes

Review Juanita's ABC notes in exhibit 2.2, and answer the questions that follow. (Suggested answers are provided in appendix G.)

EXHIBIT 2.2   **ABC notes for Juanita, a fifth-grade student**

Date, time, duration	Setting Events	Activity	Antecedent	Behavior	Consequences
12/2, 11:15 am, 2 minutes	Juanita told her homeroom teacher that she didn't like the haircut her stepmother had given her.	Science	Mr. Truffle asks her to take off her hood, saying loudly, "It's not a choice."	Juanita puts her middle finger up at Mr. Truffle.	She is told to go to the office, which she does.
12/4, 12:30 pm, 4 minutes		Math	Ms. Nguyen breaks up the students into five groups to do a math project.	Juanita says she isn't going to be in the stupid group and won't sit at the table with her assigned group.	She is told to work with the group, or go see the counselor. She goes to see the counselor.
12/11, 11:50 am, 4 minutes		Lunch	Juanita is told she can't go to the bathroom until a peer returns (one student allowed at a time).	Juanita calls the lunch monitor a "beast" and goes to the bathroom anyway.	The principal is called and meets Juanita in the hallway; the principal asks her to go to the office for the remainder of lunch.
12/18, 2:00 pm, 37 minutes	Juanita's social worker reported that the police were called to her house over the weekend for a domestic disturbance.	English	Ms. Hernandez tells Juanita to edit the story she wrote the previous day.	Juanita puts her head down and seems to be sleeping.	Ms. Hernandez wakes her at the end of class.
12/19, 2:00 pm, 1 minute	Juanita's biological mother contacted Juanita the night before saying she would be in town for the holidays.	English	Ms. Hernandez says, "Good afternoon," when Juanita enters the classroom.	Juanita mimics the teacher's "good after*noon*" and wiggles her hips.	Students laugh. Ms. Hernandez ignores her.
12/19, 2:30 pm, 4 minutes		Hallway after dismissal	A peer walks past Juanita while she's standing with three friends.	Juanita tells the peer she is a fat pig as she walks by.	Three peers standing with Juanita laugh.

Answer the following questions after looking at Juanita's ABC notes. (When analyzing data, data points can be used in more than one category.) Reviewing chapter 1 of *The Behavior Code* about function of behavior will help you answer question number five.

1. What patterns do you notice in the antecedent column?

2. What patterns, if any, do you notice with the setting events?

3. What patterns do you notice with time of day or activity?

4. What patterns do you notice in the consequence column?

5. What is your hypothesis of the function or functions of Juanita's behavior, in light of these patterns?

Using ABC Information to Inform Your Practice

Let's say you are Juanita's teacher. Use the ABC notes to inform your practice.

1. Are there any patterns with time of day or activities? If so, what interventions would you implement to address the patterns?

2. Looking at the antecedent patterns in the ABC notes for Juanita, how would you change your interventions to prevent the student from engaging in unwanted behavior in the future?

3. What do you notice about the setting events? Do you need to check in with Juanita? Do you need to report any information to the principal or social worker or student's private therapist? Are you focusing on what you can do within the school day?

4. Looking at the consequence patterns in the ABC notes, how would you change your responses in the future so that you do not reinforce the function of Juanita's behavior?

Analyzing Raul's ABC Notes

Review Raul's ABC notes exhibit 2.3 and answer the questions that follow.

EXHIBIT 2.3   **ABC notes for Raul, a second-grade student**

Date, time, duration	Setting event	Activity	Antecedent	Behavior	Consequence
1/25, 2:00 pm, 15 min		Chorus class	Raul is sitting with the class on the stage while the chorus teacher pulls a student aside to talk to him.	Raul walks out of the auditorium.	Peers tell the teacher, who follows Raul several minutes later. He is sent back to the classroom to wait with Ms. Chounan.
2/2, 1:15 pm, 13 minutes	Raul's mother sent in a note that said it was a "rough morning" and that Raul was crying hysterically on the way to school, saying he hates it.	Math	Ms. Chounan tells the class they need to tape their completed math sheets on the wall for display.	Raul puts his head down and does not do the math sheet.	Several times, Ms. Chounan tells him he needs to get started.
2/4, 1:30 pm, 20 minutes	Raul's mother sent Ms. Chounan an e-mail explaining that he couldn't complete his writing homework and that he got really "worked up" over it.	Language arts	Ms. Chounan tells Raul to stop writing on the laptop because it is time for reading.	Raul keeps typing his story.	Ms. Chounan tells him three more times to get off the computer and then tells him he can't use the laptop tomorrow.
2/13, 1:55 pm, 32 minutes	Raul's mother told the teacher his babysitter would be picking him up today.	Language arts	Students are coming in from art class, and the teacher tells them it is time for reading group.	Raul walks into class and sits at the back table instead of his desk.	Ms. Chounan asks him several times to sit at his desk with his reading group.
3/1, 2:55 pm, 5 minutes		Homework/organization dismissal	Ms. Chounan tells students to write down their homework, including the writing journal, and says she will come around and check it.	Raul has his head on his desk and does not take out his homework folder.	Ms. Chounan reminds him to take out his homework folder four times and then she takes it out of his desk and writes it down for him.
3/3, 2:00 pm, 3 minutes	Raul's babysitter will be picking him up today.	Extra recess	Class is out on the playground for about three minutes. Raul asks if he can get a drink of water.	Raul is sitting in the classroom when the class returns from recess.	Ms. Chounan tells Raul she is going to call his mother and that leaving recess to come to the classroom isn't safe.

After looking at Raul's ABC notes, ask yourself:

1. What patterns do you notice in the antecedent column?

2. What patterns, if any, do you notice with setting events?

3. What patterns do you notice with time of day or activity?

4. What patterns do you notice in the consequence column?

5. What is your hypothesis of the function or functions of Raul's behavior in light of these patterns?

Using ABC Information to Inform Practice

Let's say you are Raul's teacher. Use the ABC notes to inform your practice.

1. Are there any patterns with time of day or activities? If so, what interventions would you implement to address the patterns?

2. Looking at the antecedent patterns in the ABC notes for Raul, how would you change your interventions to prevent the student from engaging in unwanted behavior in the future?

3. What do you notice about the setting events? Do you need to check in with Raul? Do you need to report any information to the principal or social worker or the student's private therapist? Are you focusing on what you can do within the school day?

4. Looking at the consequence patterns in the ABC notes, how would you change your responses in the future so that you do not reinforce the function of Raul's behavior?

Analyzing ABC Notes for Your Student

After documenting behavior incidents of one of your students on an ABC sheet, alone or with your team review the sheet, and answer the following questions. Remember, when you are analyzing data, you can use data points in more than one category.

1. What patterns do you notice in the antecedent column?

2. What patterns, if any, do you notice with setting events?

3. What patterns do you notice with time of day or activity?

4. What patterns do you notice in the consequence column?

5. What is your hypothesis of the function or functions of the student's behavior, in light of these patterns?

Using ABC Information to Inform Your Practice

Use the notes you have compiled for your own student to answer the following questions:

1. Are there any patterns with time of day or activities? If so, what interventions are you going to implement to address the patterns?

2. Looking at the antecedent patterns in the ABC notes you've taken for your student, how will you change your interventions to prevent the student from engaging in unwanted behavior in the future?

3. What do you notice about the setting events? Do you need to check in with the student? Do you need to report any information to the principal or social worker or the student's private therapist? Are you focusing on what you can do within the school day?

4. Looking at the consequence patterns in the ABC notes you've taken for your student, how will you change your responses in the future so that you do not reinforce the function of the student's behavior?

Structured ABC Data Sheet

Directions: The teacher will tailor structured data sheet to reflect common ante-cedents, behaviors, and consequences demonstrated by the student. When the teacher observes a behavior incident, check the box that best describes what was observed or check "other" and write the information (the data collector may check off multiple boxes in each column).

Student: _____

Date, time, duration	Setting event	Activity	Antecedent (what is happening in environment immediately before the behavior occurs)	Behavior (describe the behavior of student)	Consequence (staff or environmental reaction immediately after behavior)
			☐ Asked to stop activity: _____ ☐ Asked to start activity: _____ ☐ Transition through the hallways ☐ Interacting with peer ☐ Whole class lesson (where: _____) ☐ Other:	☐ Noncompliance ☐ Yelling ☐ Other:	☐ Teacher *ignores* behavior. ☐ Peer *ignores* behavior. ☐ Peer *pays attention* to student (either positive attention or negative attention). ☐ Teacher repeats *verbal directions* until student complies ☐ Student successfully avoids work (doesn't do work) ☐ Other:
			☐ Asked to stop activity: _____ ☐ Asked to start activity: _____ ☐ Transition through the hallways ☐ Interacting with peer ☐ Whole class lesson (where: _____) ☐ Other:	☐ Noncompliance ☐ Yelling ☐ Other:	☐ Teacher *ignores* behavior. ☐ Peer *ignores* behavior. ☐ Peer *pays attention* to student (either positive attention or negative attention). ☐ Teacher repeats *verbal directions* until student complies ☐ Student successfully avoids work (doesn't do work) ☐ Other:
			☐ Asked to stop activity: _____ ☐ Asked to start activity: _____ ☐ Transition through the hallways ☐ Interacting with peer ☐ Whole class lesson (where: _____) ☐ Other:	☐ Noncompliance ☐ Yelling ☐ Other:	☐ Teacher *ignores* behavior. ☐ Peer *ignores* behavior. ☐ Peer *pays attention* to student (either positive attention or negative attention). ☐ Teacher repeats *verbal directions* until student complies ☐ Student successfully avoids work (doesn't do work) ☐ Other:
			☐ Asked to stop activity: _____ ☐ Asked to start activity: _____ ☐ Transition through the hallways ☐ Interacting with peer ☐ Whole class lesson (where: _____) ☐ Other:	☐ Noncompliance ☐ Yelling ☐ Other:	☐ Teacher *ignores* behavior. ☐ Peer *ignores* behavior. ☐ Peer *pays attention* to student (either positive attention or negative attention). ☐ Teacher repeats *verbal directions* until student complies ☐ Student successfully avoids work (doesn't do work) ☐ Other:

CHAPTER 3

Key Interventions for Successfully Supporting Students

In this chapter, we will practice implementing and assessing key interventions that can be used both for students with anxiety-related behavior and those with oppositional behaviors. The *accommodations* component of the FAIR Behavior Intervention Plan will be discussed: transitions, breaks, and alternative lunch and recess. Relationship building and validation, two *interaction* strategies (the *I* in FAIR) that are universally helpful for students with challenging behavior, will also be discussed.

Smooth transitions from one activity to another are critical to school success and often require accommodations such as specific transition warnings, strategies for staying calm during downtime, and support for initiating a task. Breaks and alternative lunch and recess are also critical accommodations that teachers often have questions about and wish to practice, as these events are logistically difficult to implement and often are not calming for the student. We will unpack the logistical and clinical factors that make these accommodations successful so that students benefit, feel calm and successful, and are more open to learning and participating throughout the day.

TRANSITIONS: REVIEW

Transitions are among the most difficult times of the day for some students with anxiety or oppositional behavior, because these situations require many skills, including flexibility and executive functioning skills. There are four components to every transition, and it's important to choose an appropriate warning for each component:

- *The cessation of the first activity:* Give a concrete transition warning (instead of a countdown warning, which doesn't help students stop an activity). Find a stopping place (e.g., place a note that says "Stop reading" at the end of the chapter, or tell the student, "Five more bites, then it's time to be finished").
- *A cognitive shift to the next activity:* Help the student visualize the new activity. Take a photograph of the student (if younger), or use a visual schedule with an older student.
- *The actual start of the next activity:* The countdown transition warning will help students learn when the next activity will start (e.g., "We are going to finish math and start science in five minutes"). The countdown warning to prompt stopping doesn't work as well as a countdown to the next activity. The countdown to stopping requires a student to stop in midstream, which is difficult, especially for inflexible students. On the other hand, the countdown to the start of an activity clearly communicates the expected start time of an activity and can be helpful.
- *The lack of inherent structure and specific expectations during the transition time:* When a transition has a lot of waiting time (e.g., with a whole-class transition), use structured, concrete tasks as time and energy "sponges" (e.g., have a student fold papers, clean the chalkboard, or push in chairs to keep him productive and discourage him from becoming dysregulated).

TRANSITIONS: EXPANDED

In school, we ask students to make transitions frequently and with little support. Difficulty with transition is at the root of many incidents of noncompliance. When students "don't stop reading when asked," "never follow directions," or "have to be chased to come in from recess," these incidents of noncompliance can be symptoms of a more fundamental problem with transitions. We may be asking students to do something they do not have the skills to execute.

The Behavior Code describes appropriate transition warnings for each stage of a transition. But what do we do when transition warnings are not enough and the student is still resisting? We also need to provide accommodations and build transition skills.

Stopping the Activity

Students have difficulty stopping an activity they are in the midst of. They may need explicit instruction about how to pick an activity that is a good match for the time allotted (e.g., pick a short computer game when you only have five minutes) and how to find a stopping place before they begin (e.g., "I will stop reading when I reach chapter 3"). If possible, avoid activities that are too reinforcing if possible during the school day; students will have a hard time stopping an activity that they really love. Asking a student to play a favorite video game for only ten minutes is often a setup for a problem, so it may be best not to give that as an option during school. If the student is consistently having trouble stopping an activity, arrange the schedule so that a preferred activity occurs afterward. For example, you might say, "Time to stop the computer math game and have a snack."

Tales from the Field

Gail, a first-grade student with anxiety, was enjoying a large muffin for snack time. Her teacher did a countdown and said that snack time was over. Gail, who was only halfway done with her muffin, verbally refused: "I don't think so." The teacher tried giving her warnings and even threatened to take away recess, to no avail (the student just became more agitated and began yelling). The following day, Gail came in with a similarly sized muffin. Before she started to eat, the teacher said, "Let's find a stopping place. You have time for half your muffin." Gail put the other half of her muffin away and made the transition successfully at the end of snack time.

Cognitive Shift

Students have to make a mental shift before a physical one. They have to stop thinking about snack time and start thinking about science. The shift includes visualizing what being ready for science looks like (e.g., the student sitting at her desk with her science notebook out). Video modeling (having students watch a video of a student or themselves transitioning well) can be a good way to preview and create a visual picture of the next activity in the transition. See the box "Taking Advantage of Technology" at the end of the "Transitions, Expanded" section for apps that create a future picture of the student as well as video modeling apps.

> **Tip** To promote a smooth cognitive shift, involve the student in creating the visuals, photographs, or videos used for making a transition. This will help buy-in and help them remember the visual.

Starting the Next Activity

Anxiety significantly affects a person's ability to initiate an activity. Any of us who have procrastinated on writing a report can identify with the instinct to avoid a perceived difficult task. Traditional approaches such as incentivizing the student to do work (e.g., "You can get an extra five minutes of recess for every math paper you finish") may not be effective. In addition to countdown transition warnings, many students also need help to begin the new activity. Accommodations are often necessary for a student to initiate, yet we are typically not supporting initiation in school.

Avoidance of a task, an inherent, protective response to a stressor, is the flight part of the fight-flight-or-freeze anxiety response. This anxious response is escape motivated and could be a result of the student's anxious thinking ("I am horrible at this!" "I stink at math"). Consequently, positive, factual thinking and thought stopping might be important skills that have been underdeveloped in students and need to be explicitly taught.

Helping Students Start

As teachers, we typically give students work, and then, moments later, when we notice that a student hasn't started, we offer help. For students with anxiety, I would propose a more errorless approach. If you as a teacher only have thirty seconds for each student, make it the first thirty seconds. Many students require support to initiate a task when they are anxious. Help them get started.

> **Tip** If you don't have the first thirty seconds to two minutes to help the student, you can give the student a warm-up or waiting activity such as a crossword puzzle until you have a minute to help him or her start. Such an activity prevents the student from sitting in front of the assignment, waiting for ten minutes and becoming increasingly anxious. By the time you get to them at that point, the student is probably highly anxious and has irreparably shut down.

It's important to rule out other causes of a student's inability to start a task quickly. Perhaps the teacher's directions weren't clear. You can do a comprehension test to check this. Ask the student, "What were the directions?" Or the student might need time to have his ideas incubate before a writing assignment. Or perhaps a student with obsessive tendencies needs to make sure her materials are arranged or put away before she starts.

Tales from the Field

Carlos, a first-grade student with the diagnosis of generalized anxiety and separation anxiety, was off to a great start in the school year, despite his chronic oppositional and explosive behavior in kindergarten. But after Thanksgiving break, Carlos started to have an increase in noncompliant behavior and began to refuse to do work, particularly writing.

I recommended that the teacher help Carlos get started by writing the first sentence of his story for him and using a sentence starter ("I went to the beach with _____") for the second sentence before she walked away. This one intervention turned the tide for this student. He began to complete writing assignments and made the transition to writing from other activities without resistance. After a few weeks, the teacher weaned Carlos off this support, and he was able to initiate with minimal check-ins from the teacher.

Many teachers worry that by helping a student get started, the student will become dependent on the help and won't learn to initiate. Anxious, all-or-nothing thinking such as "I hate math! I am horrible at spelling!" can be at the root of a lack of initiation. When we help students start and support their initiation over time, they will gain confidence and a more positive association with that subject matter.

Sentence starters are a great way to help a student start writing. Start writing the sentence for the student, and then hand the student the pencil.

Previewing

We can't preview enough for students with anxiety. Most teachers will review a visual schedule of the school day with their students in the morning. This is an excellent way to help students predict and prepare for the agenda of the day.

However, it doesn't necessarily mitigate a student's anxiety toward a particular subject and often doesn't help them initiate the activity when it comes time. If a student is anxious about math, for example, telling him math will be at 10:30 a.m. doesn't necessarily reduce his anxiety and may even make him anxious all morning in anticipation. As a supplement to reviewing the schedule, preview the actual piece of work they will be asked to do: "Here is the math sheet we will be doing today. Let's do the first problem together." Then when math class comes, the student has an entry point and will be less likely to have an initial avoidance response.

 When reviewing an actual piece of work for the students, emphasize that they don't have to do the assignment right then and that it's only a preview: "We are not going to do math right now—you don't have to do math until much later in the day—but I just wanted to really quickly show you what we are going to do."

 Previewing a lesson the day before or the first thing in the morning will help a struggling student feel more on top of the content in a challenging subject area during the actual lesson.

 Reminding a student of specific instances of past success is an empowering strategy during a preview.

If you are concerned that previewing will take too much time, consider using homework as a preview. We often use homework to review concepts that students have learned that day, but it can also be used as a preview. For example, you might tell the students, "Start the first two sentences of the story you will write in class tomorrow." An assignment like this may help the struggling student enter class with more confidence to get started. Another solution if you are not able to preview the actual work in the morning is to do it at any point during class in preparation for the following day: "We are going to do this tomorrow. Let's start it now."

 If students are struggling with homework completion, helping them start their homework in school will be a significant help.

Some students get so anxious in the beginning of an anxiety-provoking subject, they feel the need to be physically out of the room. Allowing a student to observe the beginning of the lesson while outside the classroom can allow her to hear the directions and the agenda of the class while feeling protected. Often, students will decide to join the class after hearing the instruction and directions. I had one sobbing student watch the teacher's explanation of an activity from the comfort of the hallway using a video-sharing app, FaceTime, only to have him stop crying and say, "Oh, that's not so bad" and rejoin the class.

REFLECT

Supporting Student Work Initiation

Think of a student you have who is having difficulty starting work. Consider the following questions:

1. What strategies have you used to help your student start?

2. Which of these ideas are you going to try? Why?

3. Do you worry that if you help the student start, you are overhelping and the student might become dependent?

4. Without supporting initiation, what might happen to the student's avoidance behavior over time? What might happen to the student's work production?

Making the Transition to a Nonpreferred Activity

One of the most difficult transitions for a student is going from a preferred activity to a nonpreferred one (e.g., "Please shut off the computer and come do your math quiz"). Not only must the student stop a fun and preferred activity, but they then needs to initiate a dreaded activity. We may be asking students to do something that they don't have the skills to execute. This task is like jumping off a cliff into cold water. It's easier to ease into the water by wading in. Getting off the computer is hard enough; then to immediately have to do something difficult is a setup for resistance. Instead, have the student step down and shift more gradually from a preferred to a less preferred to a nonpreferred activity—no longer a cliff but a sloping beach, as illustrated in figure 3.1. This practice will require less shifting and less flexibility on the part of the student.

FIGURE 3.1   **Abrupt versus gradual transitions**

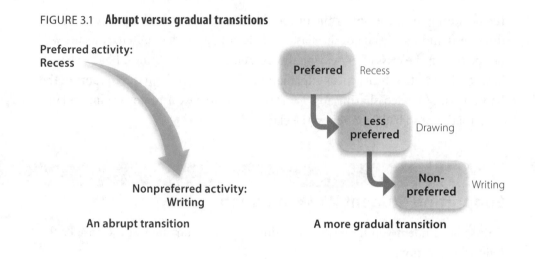

An abrupt transition

A more gradual transition

Tales from the Field

John was a kindergarten student who was starting to show a lot of noncompliance. He began to be aggressive coming in from recess and would even hide in the playground structure, requiring the teacher and the assistant teacher to take up to twenty minutes coaxing him out. After reviewing the ABC data, we saw that John's recess often came directly before writing, setting up the scenario where he had to leave recess and come in to write, which he expressed hating.

Through his behavior, John was communicating that he needed support to make this transition.

Just changing the transition warning to "Find a stopping place" helped him stop playing, but he still wouldn't come inside. Leaving recess, which he loved, to start writing, which he hated, was too abrupt for him. He needed a transition accommodation.

After asking him to find a stopping place, his teacher told him that it was time for drawing (instead of mentioning writing). John came in without a problem and sat at his desk and began to draw. Once he was sitting at the desk and had been drawing for about five minutes, the teacher then initiated a smooth transition to writing.

Tip *Use warm-ups such as crossword puzzles, word searches, and drawing—anything that the student can do at her desk, that preferably requires a writing utensil, and that is not aversive (maybe even pleasant) is a good way to start class for the student. Once at her desk, the student just needs to make the smaller transition from warm up to work. This technique can be done with the whole class as well.*

Tip *Another gradual transition into work is for students to start with easy work and move toward more difficult work. Starting with easy or below-grade-level work in the beginning of class will allow the student to ease in, or ramp up, to the activity, gain confidence, and develop behavioral momentum.[1] The concept behind this strategy is that compliant behavior on an easier task increases the likelihood of more compliant behavior on other tasks.*

Tip *Another way to provide a gradual transition is to embed a leadership activity or task, if the student likes such tasks. You might ask, for example, "Stephen, can you come in from recess and help me sharpen pencils?" Then while he's sharpening, ask him to take his pencil to his desk, without mentioning the nonpreferred activity until he's sitting. Mentioning math while he's at recess will be a setup for resistance.*

REFLECT

Transitions and Your Students

Think of a student who has difficulty with transitions. Answer the following questions:

1. What are some of his or her nonpreferred activities?

2. What are some preferred activities?

3. Is the student currently required to make the transition from preferred to non-preferred activities during the day?

Explicit Instruction for Initiation

To see long-term behavior change, a teacher needs to teach students that initiation (getting started on their own) is a challenge or a missing skill for them and that by using some helpful strategies and explicit instruction, the students can move toward long-term behavior change and independence. This knowledge is also empowering. A student who realizes, "I only have a problem getting started" faces a challenge less overwhelming and more achievable than if the student thinks, "I can't do math." Here are some ideas for teaching initiation:

- *Social stories:* stories that describe a situation, skill, or concept in terms of relevant social cues, perspectives, and common responses[2]
- *Video modeling:* a mode of teaching that uses videos to provide a visual model of the targeted behavior or skill[3]
- *Role-play:* acting out solutions to common problems
- *Positive thinking:* empowering statements or thoughts that can reduce resistance when negative, anxious thoughts prevent students from starting
- *Images of strategies:* photographs, videos, or other visual images illustrating the statement "When I can't start and feel overwhelmed, I can . . ."
- *Self-monitoring strategies:* a checklist of strategies that help the student start and keep track of which strategies are helpful

Tales from the Field

Ben's third-grade teacher, Ms. Fieldman, described Ben as pacing around the room or going to the hallway for a drink or going to the bathroom for about 80 percent of the school day. He would cry and flop to the floor if pushed to do work. He verbalized a helpless attitude toward work: "I can't do it!" and "I can't do anything!" One thing Ben *did* love to do was sudoku puzzles. Allowing Ben to start with a warm-up puzzle before every class meant that he was able to enter class and sit in his seat. Ms. Fieldman then began to help him start each assignment, which led to a 70 percent increase in work production. After a few months, she started to teach him to advocate for strategies that helped him start, and Ben began to ask for help or get pictures from the Internet to help him think of an idea for writing. By the end of the year, his helpless and overwhelmed language improved, and he would occasionally say, "I need help starting" instead of "I can't do it!"

Transition Object

Sometimes a simple statement like "It's time for chorus" can elicit an oppositional response. The statement is a direct demand. To make this direction less overwhelming and easier to respond to, a teacher may offer a transition object. Instead of focusing the direction on the less preferred activity (e.g., "Let's go to chorus"), shifting the emphasis on a small, interim task can promote compliance. So instead of saying, "Let's go to chorus," ask the student, "Can you bring this notebook to the chorus teacher?" This direction is much more palatable to the student, as it is a discrete, achievable step, as opposed to the idea of going to chorus, which can feel overwhelming (e.g., "What am I going to have to do?" "What if I have to sing in front of kids?" "What if I have to hear that song I hate?"). Once the student completes the task (delivers the notebook), he will often find himself already involved in the class activity. Transition objects can get students over the hump of initiating an overwhelming transition.

 Comfort items, such as a tiny stuffed animal from home or a favorite bracelet, can help students make the transition to an anxiety-provoking activity.

Support for Waiting or Down Time

Over the years, I have analyzed nearly every facet of student behavior and every minute of the school day. Not surprisingly, students often have difficulty during downtime or wait time. In *The Behavior Code*, transition sponges and waiting bags were described as helpful accommodations during difficult downtime. But before a student can use these strategies, we need to teach her to identify wait time or downtime. Unfortunately, the world doesn't announce these times; they just occur. Through the use of social stories, videos, examples and nonexamples, or role-play, we can explicitly teach the student how to recognize that downtime is beginning.

While the student is learning to identify downtime, use a consistent prompt such as "look around" to encourage the student to observe the cues of downtime. Whenever possible, it would also be very helpful for the classroom teacher to announce that it is wait time and to remind the whole class what the students can do while they wait. For example, "We have to wait for a few minutes. This would be a good time to silently review the lyrics of the song you will be singing in chorus later."

For students in second through sixth grade, waiting bags or fidget toys might be supplemented or replaced with cognitive waiting strategies such as thinking of the lyrics of a favorite song or mentally reviewing multiplication facts.

Tip With younger students (grades K–3), I've learned to teach them that they will get in less trouble when they're sitting than when they are standing. Being seated puts more structure and boundaries on where their body is in space. This sitting strategy can be used with the whole class: have all the students sit at their seats, and call only a few students at a time to line up so that they are not all getting up at the same time. In the hallway, if you're waiting for the cafeteria to clear out or PE to be ready, having the class sit against the wall will keep the students more regulated overall.

Tip For students who can't wait to be called on and frequently call out, you can hold up a sign that says raise your hand or, for young grades, that has a picture of a student raising a hand. This great concrete reminder also benefits others in the class.

Taking Advantage of Technology

To use video modeling as a tool for helping students with transitions, obtain parental parent permission and then record a student role-playing an appropriate transition or demonstrating an appropriate transition in real time. See the sections "Video Modeling" and "Creating Stories to Teach Strategies and Social Skills" in appendix C for more transition skills.

When a student is having trouble entering the room, use a video-sharing app, FaceTime, Skype, or other ways for the student to participate in the class remotely. Virtual meeting apps like those at Edmoto.com and Wiggio.com also offer possibilities.

The section "Executive Functioning" in appendix C lists apps that help students create a future picture. Electronic timers and timer apps can help support transitions for some students.

Xavier, a Fourth-Grade Student

Read the following scenarios, and using exhibit 3.1, answer the questions about Xavier's transition.

> Xavier was allowed to go on the computer during indoor recess. Ms. Parker announced that recess would be over in five more minutes and then the class would start writing. Even after the teacher gave a countdown warning and made several other attempts to shift him, Xavier refused to get off the computer. Ms. Parker told Xavier that she had asked him several times to get off the computer and that he wasn't listening to directions. She then told him he was not going to have access to the computer the next day, since he was not proving he could handle the privilege.
>
> Xavier did not get off the computer and sit down at his desk until his game ended, ten minutes into writing class. He sat at his desk and stared out the window. Ms. Parker told Xavier that he was wasting time and that he needed to take out a pencil. After fidgeting with the contents of his desk, Xavier announced that his pencil was missing. Ms. Parker gave him a new pencil. He wrote his name on his paper and then asked to go to the bathroom. Ms. Parker said he could go. Eight minutes later, Xavier returned to class, sat down, and immediately got back up and retrieved a tissue from the tissue box across the room. He walked back to his desk and sat there fidgeting with his shoelace for the next five minutes. Ms. Parker asked the students if any volunteers wanted to read their story to the class. Xavier asked if he could go to the bathroom. Ms. Parker said he needed to wait.

Consider the following questions about this series of events:

1. The countdown transition warning wasn't effective to help Xavier stop playing the computer. Why? What transition warning would you recommend for him?

2. Would Xavier benefit from some cognitive shifting support? If so, what are some clues that suggest this? Which types of support would you use?

3. Xavier was able to write his name on his paper independently, but then produced no work for the rest of the period. How would you support Xavier's initiation? Would a transition warning be enough? Does he need accommodations? If so, which ones?

4. Does Xavier have difficulty during downtime? What are some clues that suggest this?

5. Does Xavier require explicit instruction around transitions? If so, which part or parts of the transition does he require instruction in, and how would you teach these skills?

Trevor, a First-Grade Student

Trevor is a first-grade student in foster care because of extreme neglect in his previous home. He has difficulty walking in the hallway and entering the class appropriately, and he is a year below grade level in math. On one particular day when the class was leaving PE (one of Trevor's favorite classes), Trevor lined up and left the gym nicely. But then in the hallway on the way to math class, he stepped out of line; ran past both his class and his teacher, Mr. Shin; and entered the classroom. Trevor climbed on top of a table and was jumping from one table to another, saying, "Look at me!" Mr. Shin told Trevor to get down and told the other students to sit in their seats. Trevor then grabbed a bin of math manipulatives off a table and tipped it over, yelling, "No math today!"

Let's examine these events:

1. Does Trevor have difficulty stopping the activity? If so, what are some clues that suggest this?

2. Does Trevor have difficulty cognitively shifting? If so, what are some clues that suggest this? What types of support would be helpful?

3. Trevor had difficulty entering the classroom. How would you support Trevor's initiation? Would a transition warning be enough? Does he need accommodations? If so, which ones?

4. Does Trevor have difficulty during downtime? If so, what are some clues that suggest this? What support might be helpful?

5. Does Trevor require explicit instruction around transitions? If so, what and how would you explicitly teach Trevor so he can learn to make transitions?

Making a Transition Support Plan

Think of a student you are working with who is having difficulty with transitions, and use exhibit 3.1 to make a plan by filling in the last two columns.

EXHIBIT 3.1   **Transition support chart**

Part of the transition	Transition warnings	Transition accommodations	Explicit instruction	What has been tried	Next steps; notes
Stopping the first activity	• "Find a stopping place" • "You have time for [insert amount]" • Other:	• Graduated transition activity: add a warm-up activity, leadership task, or preferred activity • Limit optional highly preferred activities • Time non-preferred activity so it's prior to preferred activity • Use visual timers so the students can judge if they have time to start a new game, etc. • Provide an agreed-upon stopping place before starting the activity • Other:	• Teach student how to find a stopping place before starting an activity • Teach and practice with student how to pick an appropriate activity for the time allotted • Rehearsal and practice of transitions • Video modeling • Social stories • Comic strips • Teach student to ask for "one more minute" rather than act out • Other:		
Cognitive shift to the next activity	• "Picture the next activity" • "What materials are you going to need for science?" • "For the next activity, you will be [location], and will need X" • Other:	• Transition object • Use photograph or visual support as a reminder • Self-talk: repeat "being ready for science means . . ." • Other:	• Rehearsal and practice of transitions • Video modeling • Social stories • Comic strips • Other:		

(continues)

Part of the transition	Transition warnings	Transition accommodations	Explicit instruction	What has been tried	Next steps; notes
Actual start of the next activity	• Countdown • Include specifics about materials needed, location, and behavior expectations • "In a minute, we will get our blue math folders and sit at our desks quietly" • Other:	• Transition object • Preview (specify how and what) and help student start work ahead of time • Help students start • Graduated transition activity: add a warm up activity, leadership task, or preferred activity • Graduated transition activity: Easy work first • Other:	• Psychoeducation: "You have trouble starting an activity" • Self-monitor with strategy list: "When I have trouble starting, I can . . ." (e.g., ask for help, engage in positive thinking) • Rehearsal and practice of transitions • Video modeling • Social stories • Comic strips • For students refusing to enter class: observe the beginning of the lesson while outside the room using technology (e.g., FaceTime, Skype, Edmoto) • Other:		
The lack of inherent structure and specific expectations during transition time	• "It's time to wait, you can . . ." (give structural choices) • "It's downtime" • Other:	• Younger kids: wait bag or wait fidgets • Older students: doodle, engage in a cognitive task: think of song lyrics, math facts • Cheat sheet (small card with a list of waiting strategies) • Transition sponges	• Social story or role-play about how to know you are being asked to wait • Rehearsal and practice of transitions • Video modeling • Social stories • Comic strips • Other:		

BREAKS: REVIEW

All intervention plans for students with anxiety-related and oppositional behavior need to consider including breaks throughout the day. Breaks are an important accommodation for many students. When breaks are given preventatively (i.e., the break is *not* earned) throughout the day, either on a set schedule or as needed, they can help the students avoid being overcome with anxiety over time and can deter inappropriate behavior. Proper timing and the content of the break depend on the individual student.

For students with oppositional behavior, we need to remember they are constantly asked to shift from their agenda to engage in less preferred activities and to comply with authority, which may be exceptionally difficult for them. They benefit from breaks, which help them refuel and can prevent outbursts. Unfortunately, breaks are often underused for students with oppositional behavior. The breaks need to highlight an escape from demands (which they are required to comply with all day) and allow them to feel "in charge."

BREAKS: EXPANDED

The major goal of any break is to help the student be more regulated after the break. While this goal sounds obvious, it is often not the case. In fact, many teachers set up the break as a reward, so the break does not achieve the desired result. It is also important to choose the right type of activity for the individual student. For some students, for example, the teacher might need to consider whether they would be helped by a cognitively distracting activity or an activity that helps others.

Tip *Because students will often request a break when they are anxious, they may find it more difficult to verbally express themselves. A break card can be a helpful way for them to communicate without the verbal requirement. Having the student make the break card with the teacher can be a nice way to elicit buy-in.*

Tip *Creating a hierarchy of break cards is a great way to help a student learn to self-monitor his needs. The student and teacher could make a quick five-minute break, a ten-minute break, and, for severely anxious kids, an opt-out-of-class break card. Most students don't actually use this last card; the mere knowledge that they can leave when they need to reduces their anxiety.*

Preventative Accommodations, Not Rewards

Teachers often confuse breaks with rewards, but students with anxiety need breaks as preventative accommodations, in the same way that students with vision problems need glasses to see—they don't need to "earn" their glasses.[4] Sometimes teachers worry that letting a student take a break is letting her get away with avoiding a task and can be perceived as the wrong approach. This concern can prevent teachers from allowing students to take breaks when they need them to prevent anxiety from escalating.

Tales from the Field

Ms. Patel conscientiously followed Mark's FAIR Behavior Intervention Plan and agreed on his need for breaks, as she had seen how he would shut down when pushed through an assignment. She even helped Mark design and laminate a break card. One day, however, Ms. Patel was helping Mark with his assignment and when he held up his handmade break card, she said, "Oh, great job using your card. Now, do just two more problems, and you can go." Her long-standing use of breaks as a reward interfered with her relatively recent awareness of breaks as a necessity, and she accidentally resorted to her former way of thinking.

Choosing the Right Activity

Movement breaks are what we commonly think of when we give a student a break. We need to be cautious about a one-size-fits-all approach to breaks. Sometimes these types of breaks are unstructured (e.g., taking a walk), and unstructured time is often a stressful time for students with anxiety. Also, many students become dysregulated or too excited when they have an opportunity for a lot of movement. Either avoid breaks that involve movement for these students, or end the movement activity with a calming activity so that the students are regulated and can rejoin the class. Teaching and modeling break activities with the student is necessary for a student to use break time effectively.

Tip *Avoid considering PE class or recess a break (e.g., "Johnny, you don't need a break; we just had recess!"). For many students, the unstructured nature of recess, the performance demands in PE, and the social demands of both provoke anxiety. This is also true for snack time and lunch.*

Tip *Students who bolt out of the classroom when they are anxious may need a break that allows them to escape the actual environment. They can take a break either outside the classroom in a designated spot or in the classroom but behind a visual barrier (e.g., a study carrel or, for younger students, a tent).*

Evaluating Breaks with Data

Finding the right strategy or activity to engage in during a break is like finding the perfect pair of shoes—you may have to try on many before you find a fit. The goal is finding a strategy that has a regulating effect. Teachers should collect data before the student engages in the activity and then afterward. If the student is calmer afterward, it is a good break choice. See exhibit 3.2 for a breaks data sheet and exhibit 4.7 for a student's self-evaluation data sheet.

Biofeedback is the use of electronic monitoring (usually a sensor on the finger connected to a mobile device or computer) to teach a person how to control the body's responses, such as heart rate. Biofeedback apps and software are a great way to have students collect data on their physiological state before and after a break and to help them know if "it worked." This technology can translate the abstract concept of calming down into concrete visual information that can help students learn faster and calm down more readily. Some students use biofeedback as a break activity, asking for a biofeedback break, as it is so effective. See "Taking Advantage of Technology" at the end of the "Breaks, Expanded" section for more information and suggestions about biofeedback.

REFLECT

Evaluating Breaks in Your Classroom

Consider the breaks in your own classroom, and answer these questions to see how well you are evaluating their effectiveness for your students:

1. How do you currently assess whether a break has been helpful for students who may need them in your classroom?

2. Are you collecting data on break effectiveness currently?

3. Are there any barriers preventing you from collecting data on breaks? Can you think of a solution to those barriers?

Break Menu or Visual List

Once you find strategies that the data show help the students regulate themselves, create a visual list or menu of break options for the student, such as the one in appendix E of *The Behavior Code*. By having a large list of ideas, the student can avoid choosing strategies that are unhelpful. For example, as mentioned, movement breaks are commonly used in schools, but not all movement is helpful.

 Tip Post the visual list of break strategies near the designated calming space or the student's seat so that student can use it as a cue when she is upset.

Tip Some students may prefer to use coping cards. These cards are like a deck of playing cards, but each coping card has a specific type of break written on it. The teacher would help the student choose an activity that is written on the card. Instead of using a general break card, these are more specific, such as a "listen to music" card.

Cognitive Distraction Breaks

When it is difficult to find a break that is regulating, the students' anxious thinking (ruminating) may be an important component of their dysregulation. Without giving the students a *cognitively distracting* break that lets them take a break from their own thoughts, the teacher cannot help them regulate themselves. Most movement and sensory breaks do not include a break from anxious or otherwise negative thinking. Watching a movie, reading a book, or meditating may be helpful cognitively distracting activities. One activity that is incompatible with having a separate anxious thought is for the student to read out loud to herself (because she can't do both at the same time, the reading interrupts the anxious thinking). Unlike reading aloud alone, reading aloud in front of others can provoke anxiety and should be avoided. Have the student choose a book at her independent level, if she is reading aloud. Otherwise, reading aloud could be frustrating.

Here are some possibly effective cognitive distraction tools or activities that are easily accessed in most classrooms:

- Videos
- Reading a book silently or aloud to yourself
- Listening to an electronic book
- Meditation
- Sudoku or word puzzles
- Mad Libs
- Trivia cards and fun fact books
- Helping others
- Leadership tasks

As the preceding list shows, another possible cognitive distraction is helping others. When a student has been anxious for a long time, he becomes very ego-centric in his perceptions, thinking, and behavior.[5] As another form of cognitive distraction, helping another person gives students a break from thinking about themselves and shifts their thinking to someone else in addition to building confidence. They could help another person by reading to a younger student, helping a student with a physical disability get to the cafeteria, or making posters to encourage people to support a local charity. I've seen students act as though the weight of the world was taken off their shoulders when this approach is used.

Tales from the Field

I received an e-mail from a school psychologist asking if I could consult with her about Aaliyah, a sixth-grade girl who was frequently asking to call her mother and leaving school early. Aaliyah had recently been diagnosed with an eating disorder and an anxiety disorder. Following her diagnoses, the team had implemented anxiety-reducing breaks and the counselor was checking in with her several times per day.

When I arrived at the school, the staff told me that Aaliyah was getting more anxious after lunch. This was to be expected, since she was working on eating at school. She was missing the majority of her classes by visiting the counselor or nurse, calling her mother, or insisting on going home early. After observing, I noticed that the breaks she was using while she was in class were made up of art activities. Aaliyah was an artist, so she was drawing or making bracelets during her breaks. But the breaks were not helping; she was missing more and more classes. The problem was that while she was drawing, Aaliyah was still able to think anxious thoughts about what she ate for lunch, her weight, and more.

The teacher, the school counselor, and I discussed break alternatives that would offer a cognitive distraction. At first we tried having her read, but she was not engaged enough. Aaliyah would stay on the same page for an unusually long period and reported she had "spaced out." After some trial and error, we came up with two break activities that precluded negative thinking for her: watching part of a movie and reading aloud to record a book for a younger student with dyslexia. Besides interrupting her negative thinking, reading aloud enabled Aaliyah to think of others, another form of break.

Taking Advantage of Technology

Electronic books can be a great choice for cognitive distraction. Additionally, numerous apps are available to help you and the student make the best break choices. See the following sections in appendix C:

- "Executive Functioning"
- "Self-Regulation"
- "Biofeedback"
- "Self-Monitoring and Mood Tracking"
- "Calming"

When a student in higher grades misses instruction during a break, have one student use Google Docs to take notes. When the student taking the break returns, the notes have been taken for him or her and are available on the computer or other electronic device.

When a student is having trouble entering the room, use a video-sharing app, Face Time, Skype, or other ways to participate in class remotely (e.g., Edmoto.com).

PRACTICE

Brainstorming Breaks

By yourself or with team members, brainstorm solutions to common problems teachers encounter when trying to implement breaks. If you are doing this activity as a team, discuss each answer when you are finished so that everyone can benefit from each other's ideas. Keep this in your lesson plan notebook as a solution cheat sheet. (Possible answers are provided in appendix G).

Concerns	Possible solutions or responses
1. If he takes a break, he'll be missing instruction.	
2. What if she refuses to come back to class from the break and gets upset?	
3. If I give him break cards so he can initiate breaks, he'll overuse them.	
4. Who is going to supervise the breaks? I don't have a classroom assistant.	
5. But she didn't earn it . . .	
6. He exhibited inappropriate behavior right before break time so we didn't give it to him. We didn't want to reinforce the inappropriate behavior.	
7. Is it OK to have the student do something rewarding on a break?	
8. I know she needs a break, and the breaks help her, but she refuses to go.	
9. Other?	

Evaluating Break Data

After reviewing the sample data sheet in exhibit 3.2, using the data sheet in exhibit 3.3 to track whether your student's break strategy is helping him or her regulate. As demonstrated in the sample data sheet, tailor the definitions of regulation states under 1, 2, and 3 to fit the dysregulation or behavior signs your student demonstrates. Collect data for at least five to ten instances per strategy to determine if the strategy—not other variables such as student's being sick or particularly excited one day—is working. Data should be taken at different times of day and activities when breaks were used. The columns in gray are optional but recommended.

EXHIBIT 3.2   **Breaks: sample data sheet**

Student's level of anxiety or frustration

1 — Low Level	2 — Medium Level	3 — High Level
• Student is functionally participating 80 percent of the class period • Student is visibly tense 20 percent of the class period	• Student is functionally participating 50 percent of the class period • Student is visibly tense 50 percent or more of the class period	• Student is functionally participating 20 percent of the class period • Student is visibly tense 80 percent of the class period

Date, time, activity	Before		Strategy	Time, activity returned to[a]	After		Effect length[b]
	What is the student's anxiety or frustration level right now? (circle one)	What was the student's reported anxiety or frustration level? (circle one)	What activity did the student choose?		What is the student's anxiety or frustration level after the strategy? (circle one)	What was the student's reported anxiety or frustration level? (circle one)	
6/1, 9:15, math	1 2 ③	1 2 ③	Biofeedback	At 9:25, math was ending when he returned. Students were cleaning their desks for snack time.	① 2 3	① 2 3	Next time behavioral signs of anxiety were observed was at 12:45
6/1, 12:45, literacy	1 2 ③	1 ② 3	Listening to a recorded book in the calming corner	At 12:55, Edward returned from the calming corner	1 ② 3	① 2 3	Unknown because he came back to class at 2:45 from PE showing signs of anxiety
6/1, 2:45, organiza-tion/ dismissal	1 2 ③	1 2 ③	Listening to a recorded book in the calming corner	At 2:58, the teacher told Edward it was time to go home	① 2 3	① 2 3	Unknown because he went home

[a]If student returns to a new activity and the stressful activity is over, note this here.
[b]How long after the break did the student shows the next behavior sign of anxiety or frustration (i.e., how long did the effect of the break last?)?

EXHIBIT 3.3   **Breaks: data sheet**

Student's level of anxiety or frustration

1 — Low Level	2 — Medium Level	3 — High Level

Date, time, activity	Before		Strategy	Time, activity returned to[a]	After		Effect length[b]
	What is the student's anxiety or frustration level right now? (circle one)	What was the student's reported anxiety or frustration level? (circle one)	What activity did the student choose?		What is the student's anxiety or frustration level after the strategy? (circle one)	What was the student's reported anxiety or frustration level? (circle one)	
	1 2 3	1 2 3			1 2 3	1 2 3	
	1 2 3	1 2 3			1 2 3	1 2 3	
	1 2 3	1 2 3			1 2 3	1 2 3	
	1 2 3	1 2 3			1 2 3	1 2 3	
	1 2 3	1 2 3			1 2 3	1 2 3	
	1 2 3	1 2 3			1 2 3	1 2 3	
	1 2 3	1 2 3			1 2 3	1 2 3	

[a]If student returns to a new activity and the stressful activity is over, note this here.
[b]How long after the break did the student show the next behavior sign of anxiety or frustration (i.e., how long did the effect of the break last?)?

ALTERNATIVE LUNCH AND RECESS: REVIEW

Lunch and recess can be noisy and overwhelming, and they are full of challenging social situations. Some students with anxiety can navigate these busy, stressful settings, especially with staff support, but others are not so successful. Even if the student manages to get through lunch or recess without an incident, he might be feeling overwhelmed afterward. Providing an alternative lunch or recess as an environmental accommodation with a small group may help keep the student's anxiety in check not only during lunch but also throughout the day.

ALTERNATIVE LUNCH AND RECESS: EXPANDED

Many educators and administrators have expressed difficulty in overcoming the logistics of alternative lunch and recess. Who will supervise? What physical space will we use? How do I explain it to students so that it isn't stigmatizing? The logistics can often be solved creatively with the whole team.

Most students will need both alternative lunch and recess, and it's best to have the same peer group for each to minimize transitions. Peers should be allowed to sign up for alternative lunch and recess and will be selected to join on a rotating schedule (the student with anxiety or oppositional behavior happens to always be picked). All participants should have parent permission (see a permission form in appendix C of *The Behavior Code*).

Islands of Competence

Robert Brooks discusses the importance of *islands of competence*—places and activities in which a student is competent and successful—in a student's life.[6] I've learned to ask teachers and other team members, "When and where is the student competent during the day? When and where is he experiencing success?" Sadly, for many students, the answer is "nowhere." An alternative lunch can convert an anxiety-producing, shaming, conflict-ridden, upsetting time of the day into an island of competence—a time when the student experiences social success and a calmer experience.

As we know, students can make statements that are self-defeating, in all-or-nothing terms, or catastrophic (e.g., "I have no friends," "If I go into the cafeteria, all the girls will laugh at me," "I never play with anyone at recess"). During alternative lunch and recess, teachers can take pictures of a student having successful interactions and keep them in a log (refer to chapter 5 of *The Behavior Code* for this and other positive-thinking strategies). The log can be used to help the student gain a more accurate episodic memory. The next time the student states that he has no friends, the teacher can bring out the photographs, promoting a more positive self-concept.

Tales from the Field

Sarah, a third-grade girl with posttraumatic stress disorder (PTSD), had been missing up to two hours of each school day (shutting down and crying in the special education teacher's office). When I met with Sarah's team, I asked, "In what part of the school day is she competent and successful?" The team struggled to think of times she was not anxious or activities that she did not find challenging. We immediately decided to implement an alternative lunch and recess, as many of her ruminations were around interactions during those times. After that, we took out her weekly schedule and decided to schedule successful activities or situations throughout her day, every two hours. When she entered school, she immediately did a leadership activity—feeding the goldfish. Throughout the day, she participated in other activities such as helping kindergarteners, doing errands, and being an office helper. By the end of the school year, Sarah was able to spend full days in the classroom. After spending so much time that year helping kindergarteners, Sarah told her mother that she wanted to become a teacher.

REFLECT

Finding Islands of Competence

If you are currently working with a student with anxiety or oppositional behavior, find the student's islands of competence by asking yourself the following questions:

1. When is the student feeling competent and successful during the day?

2. What parts of the day that are easy for most students are difficult for this student?

3. After answering the first two questions, are you concerned that your student is struggling for a large part if not all of the school day?

4. Are you worried about the student's perception of school? What about the student's perception of himself or herself?

5. How could you create more successful moments throughout the day?

6. Why would creating more successful moments throughout the day be important for this student?

Recommended Format and Activities for Alternative Lunch

I have learned to use the concept of lunch clubs when organizing an alternative lunch. Terms like "lunch buddies," which are also used for social skills groups, may give students a preconceived notion of what the group will be and what types of students will join, which could deter them.

Lunch clubs are based around a popular activity that the student with anxiety or oppositional behavior is good at, but which also appeals to peers (e.g., "cartooning club" or "Lego club"). Competitive games such as board or card games should be avoided for students who might find them anxiety-producing or frustrating.

 Invite more than one peer to the lunch club or recess, as just inviting one sets up a situation where she is more likely to say no.

 Don't have the student you're supporting invite students to join him, as this could set him up for rejection. The emphasis should be on the lunch club as a fun option for any student, rather than as a club for one student, so the teacher or other adult should be the one inviting students to join.

Recommended Format and Activities for Alternative Recess

Recess is a time that evokes anxiety in many students and ends in conflict with peers for students with oppositional behavior. We can't take recess away, because outdoor time is so crucial for students with any regulation issue. An alternative recess is a great solution, but educators often voice concerns about the logistics. Finding an adult to facilitate and supervise is a challenge as well. If supervision cannot be solved at the classroom level, engage the principal and others to see which staff in the building could help. If space is an issue, consider the following:

• Delineate a small space for a separate, structured activity (e.g., hopscotch) with small traffic cones, sidewalk chalk, or other markers. The teacher will decide how many students can sign up or volunteer to join.

• Consider an alternative time for recess. For example, if all the fifth-graders eat lunch and then go out to recess, have the small group (your student and two to four peers) do the opposite schedule (recess then lunch), giving them a break from that larger peer group.

 If lunch is before recess, have the students discuss and plan what structured activity they will do at recess. That way, they will more likely stay together and not dissipate into the larger group.

 Avoid competitive games (e.g., soccer, kickball) for students who may find them anxiety-provoking and frustrating. Cooperative games might be helpful (e.g., a scavenger hunt, collecting leaves, a recess gardening club).

 Many students need help navigating recess. If alternative recess is not possible on a certain day, see figure 5.2 in The Behavior Code *for suggestions on making a recess plan.*

Tales from the Field

Amir, a fourth-grade student with generalized anxiety disorder (GAD), was having a hard time getting through the school day. At a team meeting, the team discussed reducing the length of his school day, because of his escalating avoidant behaviors and over-reactiveness in the afternoons. I suggested we try alternative lunch and recess before moving to an abbreviated school day. We developed a "cartoon club" for this student. The teacher presented it neutrally, not mentioning that the club was for one student particularly, and provided a sign-up sheet. Students were thrilled to join (reminding us that the cafeteria isn't a favorite place for *many* kids). The teacher was so subtle about the group that Amir didn't even know it was for him. He even said to the teacher one day, "I hope I get picked for cartoon club next month!" During cartoon club, the teacher brainstormed with the group what activity they would do during recess and suggested many cooperative or noncompetitive games to play. The teacher changed the group once per month and took pictures throughout. After three months, Amir told his therapist that he has friends in school now, and he likes recess.

Taking Advantage of Technology

If removing the student from the cafeteria is not an option on a certain day, or if there are numerous students who are anxious in the cafeteria, playing an educational movie or show, or playing a recorded book can naturally regulate the whole group. The strategy takes away the pressure of socially interacting and serves as a cognitive distraction.

PRACTICE

Planning Islands of Competence

With your team members or by yourself, look at the classroom schedule of your student. See where you could fit into the schedule some activities that will allow the student to feel competent. Discuss whether you should put one in before or after a difficult activity. Data will help you decide what works best for your student.

PRACTICE

Brainstorming Barriers to Alternative Lunches

With your team members or alone, brainstorm solutions to common concerns teachers have when trying to implement alternative lunch. Pick a student to think about as you complete the activity, and write your solutions in the right-hand column.

EXHIBIT 3.4   **Alternative lunch brainstorming solutions sheet**

Concerns or questions	Possible solutions or responses
1. What's the best activity to base the lunch group around?	
2. Who is going to supervise the lunch? What if I don't have a classroom assistant or other available staff?	
3. Where can I hold the group?	
4. What if the student doesn't want to leave the cafeteria?	
5. What if the student doesn't finish eating lunch because the activity is so motivating?	
6. Should the student be in the cafeteria some days to practice tolerating the environment?	
7. What's the best way to invite others to join the lunch group?	

CHAPTER 4

"Get Away from Me!"

Strategies and Interventions for Students with Anxiety-Related Behaviors

When anxiety is underlying a student's behavior, it can lead to inconsistent, seemingly overreactive behavior that can be confusing to teachers. In this chapter, we will troubleshoot some common problems, practice some accommodations, learn how to write accommodations as part of the curriculum, and learn new interventions to support students with anxiety. We will start with a discussion of why traditional behavior plans don't always work for students with anxiety and analyze some traditional behavior plans for effectiveness.

Self-regulation, a key skill for maintaining appropriate behavior, requires many accommodations and explicit teaching and other practices for the student with anxiety. This chapter details the use of self-regulation accommodations such as the calming box, body checks, and self-calming practices. We will learn how teachers can encourage buy-in from a student when they provide a self-evaluation tool for the student to use to evaluate the effectiveness of certain self-calming strategies. The most effective interaction style is to notice sudden changes in each student and to intervene early. The chapter also offers an opportunity for reflection and problem solving for prioritizing which strategies to use with students.

ANXIETY DISORDERS: EXPANDED

Anxiety disorders are incredibly prevalent among children, adolescents, and adults. The disorders are the most common mental health concern among U.S. adolescents, with 31.9 percent having had an anxiety disorder in their lifetime.[1] There are different types of anxiety disorders, but they all share some common features, including a subjective feeling of discomfort or fear, behaviors of avoidance or escape, and physiological reactions such as sweating, nausea, and dizziness.[2] Exhibit 4.1 summarizes the features of these various anxiety disorders.

EXHIBIT 4.1   **DSM-5 update on anxiety disorders**

The fifth edition of the *Diagnostic and Statistical Manual of Mental Disorders* (DSM-5) was published in 2013, after the publication of *The Behavior Code*. This new version updated and changed some diagnoses; the changes to anxiety and related diagnoses can be seen in the table.

The major change in the DSM-5 is that obsessive-compulsive disorder (OCD) and post-traumatic stress disorder (PTSD) have been moved from the anxiety disorder section to the obsessive-compulsive and related disorders and trauma- and stressor-related disorders sections, respectively. Selective mutism has been moved into the anxiety disorder section. However, these disorders are closely related, and approaches to managing them in the school setting are similar.

Selected Anxiety and Related Diagnoses

Anxiety disorder	Features
Generalized anxiety disorder (GAD)	Excessive, uncontrollable anxiety and worry about a number of events or activities
Specific phobia	Persistent, unreasonable fear of a specific object or situation (e.g., flying, dogs, blood)
Social anxiety disorder (formerly called social phobia)	Marked, persistent fear or anxiety about one or more situations involving social interactions, being observed, or performing for others
Separation anxiety disorder	Excessive, persistent anxiety about separation from the home or people to whom the child is attached
Panic disorder	Recurrent, unexpected panic attacks with persistent worry about having another attack or with a change in behavior related to the attacks
Selective mutism	Consistent failure to speak in social situations (e.g., school), despite speaking in other situations

Obsessive-compulsive and related disorders	Features
Obsessive-compulsive disorder (OCD)	Recurrent, excessive, unreasonable obsessions (persistent, intrusive thoughts) and/or compulsions (repetitive behaviors) that cause distress or impairment

Trauma- and stressor-related disorders	Features
Post-traumatic stress disorder (PTSD)	Following exposure to an extreme traumatic stressor, the presence of intrusive symptoms, avoidance of related stimuli, changes in thoughts and mood, and increased arousal or reactivity

Source: Adapted from American Psychiatric Association, *Diagnostic and Statistical Manual of Mental Disorders: DSM-5*, 5th ed. (Washington, DC: American Psychiatric Association, 2013).

WHY REWARDS AND CONSEQUENCES DON'T ALWAYS HELP: REVIEW

Traditional school behavior plans focus on rewarding the appropriate behavior and using consequences for inappropriate behavior. However, for students with anxiety, this approach can fall short, because the criteria for rewarding behavior are constant, despite the student's fluctuating level of anxiety. The student's inconsistent ability to perform must be taken into account when you are creating an incentive program; you do not want to unintentionally punish the student for having an elevated level of anxiety and subsequent poor performance. Gold stars don't typically work for students with anxiety. Remember, the student *cannot* act appropriately because of anxiety; it's not that he won't. Instead, target specific strategies that the student needs to practice implementing, and make earning rewards *contingent on the student's use of these strategies* when she is frustrated.

WHY REWARDS AND CONSEQUENCES DON'T ALWAYS HELP: EXPANDED

Traditional behavior intervention plans used in classrooms are very helpful for increasing motivation when a student is able to perform the desired behavior. For example, if you offered me a hundred-dollar reward for speaking faster while teaching, I would probably be able to do that and would earn the money. However, if you instead asked me to speak in French for one hundred dollars, I would not be able to do so, even if I really wanted the hundred dollars. When a student's anxiety level is high, a lack of motivation is *not* the issue. The student is unable to perform (just as I am unable to speak French), and incentivizing doesn't change that (incentives are different from systematically used positive reinforcement, which can be helpful). In fact, worrying about trying to perform may increase the student's anxiety level.

> ### Tales from the Field
>
> Carrie, a sixth-grade student, would review her behavior rules every morning with her teacher. Carrie's rules were to raise her hand (no calling out), to come back from the bathroom within two minutes, and to follow directions the first time. She articulated that she got so nervous about meeting the goals, she would inevitably "blow it" within the first hour of school. In these instances, she would lose points toward an incentive and the teacher would tell her to try harder. This made Carrie feel anxious as well, as she believed that she was trying harder in school than most other students had to. Her anxiety usually led to another incident, and the cycle continued throughout the day.

Thus, we need to be careful not to assume that the behavior of the student with anxiety is due to a lack of motivation or to willful intent. Our focus for these students needs to shift from behavioral performance to skill development and practice. If there is a highly motivating incentive, we sometimes see short-term progress (i.e., it "works" for a week or so), but without skill building, this type of plan will not yield long-term behavior change.

Anxiety's Impact on the Brain and Behavior

The prefrontal cortex is the region of the brain that performs higher-order brain functions—often called executive functions—and is also the part of the brain that is most sensitive to stress. Executive functions allow us to manage our behavior to achieve our goals. These functions include starting, stopping, and shifting activities; emotional control; working memory; planning; organization; and self-monitoring. Stress can cause a decrease in these executive functions and, if prolonged, may even have long-term effects.[3] Working memory, that is, the ability to retain information for immediate processing (i.e., to keep in mind an event that just occurred; to bring to mind information from long-term memory; and to use this knowledge to regulate behavior, thought, and emotion), is one executive function that is heavily affected by stress.[4] The wide-ranging impact of stress on the brain, and thus on behavior, is not accounted for in many traditional behavior plans.

Lack of Flexibility

Many behavior plans emphasize and reward consistent and regulated behavior and performance—the exact skill many students with mental health disabilities lack. Needing to use a quiet voice *all* day, in *every* subject area, is inflexible and unrealistic for most students with anxiety-related behavior. These students may have inconsistent performance and behavior, which may fluctuate with the student's emotional state. As the student's anxiety and mood fluctuate, so do her ability to attend, behave appropriately, and do schoolwork. Such mood fluctuations can potentially cause a student to go from writing a two-page essay in the morning to struggling to produce a coherent sentence in the afternoon, or from being appropriate during a spelling quiz one moment to crying over an easier assignment the next. The teacher is left not knowing what to expect.

In contrast, FAIR Behavior Intervention Plans are flexible. The emphasis is on "reading" the student and reacting accordingly by prompting and teaching the student coping strategies with a focus on skill building and managing anxiety-provoking activities. Shifting from traditional school behavior intervention plans is difficult, but a flexible behavior intervention plan, which is proactive and supportive, can prevent students from becoming disruptive, disengaged, and work avoidant, leaving the teacher more available for teaching all students.

Concepts That May Be Missing in Traditional Behavior Intervention Plans

- *Teaching skills:* Traditional plans may lack a flexible plan that emphasizes *skill* development and the practice of underdeveloped skills over consistent behavior performance.
- *Prevention:* Traditional plans may fail to prevent anxiety adequately; they may lack antecedent analysis and preventative interventions to mitigate the student's anxiety in school.

Analyzing Harry's Behavior Plan

Review the behavior intervention plan provided in exhibit 4.2 for Harry, a second-grader with anxiety who has been exhibiting some aggressive behavior and inappropriate language. Then, answer the following questions (answers are provided in appendix G):

1. Are the target behaviors measurable? Do they represent behaviors that are appropriate and should be increased?

2. Is there a list of antecedents (collected from data) and corresponding interventions to reduce the student's anxiety in those activities or moments?

3. Is the functional hypothesis based on ABC notes or a functional behavior analysis, and is the hypothesis written on the plan?

4. What percentage of the plan is preventative, and what percentage is reactive?

5. Are warning signs listed?

6. Is there any consideration of the student's underdeveloped skills? Are they listed in the behavior intervention plan?

7. Is the reinforcement system focused on skill building and skill practice?

8. Is there a plan to reinforce, practice, and teach these underdeveloped skills?

9. Are replacement behaviors and strategies taught in this plan?

10. Are there any interaction strategies listed in this plan?

11. Does the plan use rewards and consequences based on behavior performance?

12. Does the plan make any assumptions about the student's ability to behave appropriately and consistently?

EXHIBIT 4.2 **Behavior intervention plan for Harry**

Student name: Harry Morton

Grade: 2

Target Behaviors

1. *Aggression:* any instance where Harry hits, kicks, or scratches another student or a teacher or pulls someone's hair (record daily frequency)

2. *Inappropriate language/screaming:* any instance where Harry raises his voice above the appropriate classroom level or uses words like "shut up" or "you smell stinky" (record frequency and duration)

Previewing

1. The teacher will review the visual schedule of the day with Harry the first thing in the morning.

2. Behavior expectations will be reviewed at the beginning of each period with the visual chart (e.g., "You need to follow school rules, and then you can earn _____ [reward specified]." Each token equals a minute of reward time.

3. Harry will choose the reward he wants to earn from several visual reward icons.

4. The visual token chart will be visible to him at all times so that he knows how much reward time he's earned.

5. A specific amount of work should be specified to him before a work session. Work sessions do not typically exceed twenty-five minutes.

6. Intermittently, the teacher will ask, "How many minutes of reward time have you earned?" to keep him motivated by the reward.

Reinforcement Program

Student behavior	Teacher response
If Harry has safe behavior and does not engage in screaming or inappropriate language for five minutes	The teacher will put a token on Harry's chart and say, "Great job following your rules, Harry!"
If Harry exhibits unsafe behavior, screams, or uses inappropriate language	The teacher will show Harry the token board and remind him of his reward.
If Harry continues to exhibit unsafe behavior, scream, or use inappropriate language	The teacher will show Harry the token board and tell him he has not earned a token. The teacher will prompt him to reengage in the activity he is supposed to be participating in.

At the end of the work period, Harry will cash in his tokens for reward time.

If Harry is unsafe to the staff or a student, his mother will be called, and he will be present when the call is made.

Analyzing Chandra's Behavior Plan

Now review the behavior intervention plan provided in exhibit 4.3 for Chandra, a fourth-grader who can call out and refuse to do work. Then, answer the following questions (answers are provided in appendix G):

1. Are the target behaviors measurable? Do they represent behaviors that are appropriate and should be increased?

2. Is there a list of antecedents (collected from data) and corresponding interventions to reduce the student's anxiety in those activities or moments?

3. Is the functional hypothesis based on ABC notes or a functional behavior analysis, and is the hypothesis written on the plan?

4. What percentage of the plan is preventative, and what percentage is reactive?

5. Are warning signs listed?

6. Is there any consideration of the student's underdeveloped skills? Are they listed in the behavior intervention plan?

7. Is the reinforcement system focused on skill building and skill practice?

8. Is there a plan to reinforce, practice, and teach these underdeveloped skills?

9. Are replacement behaviors and strategies taught in this plan?

10. Are there any interaction strategies listed in this plan?

11. Does the plan use rewards and consequences based on behavior performance?

12. Does the plan make any assumptions about the student's ability to behave appropriately and consistently?

EXHIBIT 4.3   **Behavior intervention plan for Chandra**

Student name: Chandra Jones
Grade: 4

Expected Behaviors

- Enter the classroom with needed materials
- Raise hand and wait for the teacher to call on her before sharing ideas
- Complete all classwork

Interventions for the Expected Behaviors

1. The teacher will go over behavior expectations with Chandra before Chandra enters the classroom. The teacher will have Chandra repeat the behavior expectations so that the teacher is sure the student understands.
2. The teacher will provide praise whenever Chandra is being appropriate and compliant.
3. Chandra will be provided with a graphic organizer for all writing activities.
4. The teacher will have a peer praise Chandra for appropriate behavior when possible.
5. The teacher will have Chandra carry her own point sheet so she can refer to it frequently and easily.

Reward Plan

1. If Chandra follows her rules, she will earn a point for each expected behavior each period.
2. If Chandra earns 75 percent of her possible points in a day, she can choose to play chess with Mr. Kelly or watch a TV show (for no more than fifteen minutes) in the resource room at the end of the day.
3. If Chandra is not following her rules, she will get a verbal warning from the teacher.
4. If Chandra continues to not follow her rules, she will be asked to speak to the teacher in the hallway.
5. Chandra will be asked to join the class with expected behaviors.
6. If Chandra does not follow her rules when she reenters the classroom, she will be asked to speak to Ms. Samison, the guidance counselor, and will lose a point on her point sheet.
7. If Chandra is unable to join the class and follow directions with Ms. Samison, Ms. Samison will decide if Chandra receives a lunch detention or an afterschool detention (depending if it is a day her mother can pick her up late).

Analyzing Your Student's Behavior Plan

Reflect on a behavior intervention plan or system that you've used with a student with anxiety and that resulted in minimal or no progress, and answer the following questions:

1. Are the target behaviors measurable? Do they include behaviors that are appropriate and should be increased?

2. Is there a list of antecedents (collected from data) and corresponding interventions to reduce the student's anxiety in those activities or moments?

3. Is the functional hypothesis based on ABC notes (or based on a functional behavior analysis), and is the hypothesis written on the plan?

4. What percentage of the plan is preventative, and what percentage is reactive?

5. Are warning signs listed?

6. Is there any consideration of the student's underdeveloped skills? Are they listed in the behavior intervention plan?

7. Is the reinforcement system focused on skill building and skill practice?

8. Is there a plan to reinforce, practice, and teach these underdeveloped skills?

9. Are replacement behaviors and strategies taught in this plan?

10. Are there any interaction strategies listed in this plan?

11. Does the plan use rewards and consequences based on behavior performance?

12. Does the plan make any assumptions about the student's ability to behave appropriately and consistently?

REDUCING ANXIETY ABOUT WRITING: REVIEW

Writing is often an area of increased stress for students with anxiety. This includes open-ended writing assignments; personal narratives or topics involving self-reflection; composition; and smaller writing tasks such as explaining an answer in math and, sometimes, any pencil-and-paper task. Anxious students often have difficulty coming up with an idea to write about and have problems with organization, editing, spelling (especially for perfectionistic students), grammar, and punctuation. Writing interventions used by the student will be indicated in the curriculum accommodation section of the FAIR Behavior Intervention Plan (see chapter 6 for practice creating FAIR Behavior Intervention Plans).

REDUCING ANXIETY ABOUT WRITING: EXPANDED

We are doing great work teaching writing skills in our schools: how to create a topic sentence, form paragraphs, use grammar, find your narrative voice, and so forth. We do not, however, typically address writing anxiety. Many students are debilitated by all-or-nothing perceptions and statements around writing—for example, "I am the worst writer," "I stink at writing," or "I hate writing." Once a student starts with this type of thought pattern, his anxiety is sure to rise, which typically leads to avoidance behavior. It is important to replace these unproductive, debilitating statements with a more realistic perspective on a student's writing abilities. Reducing anxious statements may reduce writing anxiety and subsequently reduces avoidant behavior. As writing and pencil-and-paper tasks are required in almost all subject areas, reducing writing anxiety is a key to student success and engagement in school.

My Writing Strategies: A Checklist for Students

The Behavior Code recommends using a checklist of writing strategies to help reduce all-or-nothing anxious thinking and statements, and I've since received many questions as to how exactly to implement this kind of checklist. See "Practice: Create a Writing Checklist" in this section for details on making a writing checklist.

Typically, the student only struggles with a few parts of writing and thus only requires a few strategies. After the activity, showing the student that he successfully completed the assignment with the use of only two strategies can start to disprove the student's all-or-nothing view of writing, eventually replacing statements like "I am the worst writer" with "I'm a good writer. I only have trouble with thinking of an idea, and I have two strategies to use for that." The checklist can also be empowering, as it encourages students to self-monitor and figure out what they need to succeed. Teaching students how to understand their own needs and to seek strategies that work will serve them well in the future.

With students who are younger or who strongly avoid writing, fill out the "My Writing Strategies" form (table 3.5 in *The Behavior* Code) for them and support them fully throughout the writing assignment. Show them what strategies you are checking off until they gain a more accurate view of their writing skills. Then they may be willing and able to do the sheet themselves.

Tales from the Field

Stephanie, a first-grade student with generalized anxiety disorder (GAD), was whining, crying, hiding under the table, and asking to call her mother throughout the day. After collecting ABC data, the teacher realized that the main anteced-ent category to these avoidance behaviors was writing, particularly open-ended writing activities. Stephanie would say, "I hate writing! Writing is too hard for me!" Stephanie's teacher began to use a writing strategies checklist with her, sitting next to her during writing assignments to help her use the list. After three weeks of using the checklist, Stephanie no longer engaged in avoidance behaviors, with the exception of some occasional whining. After three months, she no lon-ger needed the checklist and had a notable change in her language: "I'm a good writer, but I have trouble spelling. And I have strategies to help me."

Tip   *Many students, particularly students prone to perfectionism, have anxiety about spelling. It is the only part of writing that is either right or wrong, which is why many students don't want to take the risk and attempt spelling a word.*

Tip   *Students who are perfectionistic may feel more comfortable writing on a whiteboard or a computer rather than paper. Making mistakes with these tools feels less permanent: when you correct a mistake, it "goes away," whereas erasing a pencil mark still shows a bit, resulting in a paper that can no longer be "perfect."*

Rating System

Another strategy to reduce anxious thinking and statements around writing is to have the students rate the difficulty of the writing activity before and after the activ-ity (e.g., they could rate it on a scale of 1 to 5, with 1 being very easy and 5 being very difficult). Typically, before the activity, the student will rate the activity as a high number because of the student's anxious perception. After the activity, the student will typically have a more accurate perception and will pick a lower number. Keep the rating sheet (similar to the one in exhibit 4.4), and show it to the student the next time she starts to avoid a writing activity, claiming it's too difficult.[5] "You think this is a five? That's so interesting. Look, yesterday you thought it was going to be a five, and it turned out to only be a three! Let's see what happens with this assignment." After several days or weeks, this continuous rating strategy will help disprove the student's irrational idea that writing is extremely difficult.

Tip   *Have a discussion with the student after a few days (four or more will best illustrate a pattern) of using the rating sheet, and ask her what she notices. It's great to have her realize that her initial perception is often inaccurate as opposed to being told. You can guide this conclusion by using "I notice" statements. For example, "I notice the 'before' numbers seem to be higher than the 'after' numbers. Hmmm, I wonder why?" While having the conversation, you could show the student her rating sheet, like the one in exhibit 4.4.*

EXHIBIT 4.4   **Example of a student's rating sheet**

Before	After
5	3
5	2
4	2

Tip   *Have the student fill out the rating sheet. When you show him how he felt the day before, and the recording is in his own writing, it gives more credibility to the idea that in reality, the activity was not as hard as he had originally thought.*

Feelings About Writing

The visual chart in exhibit 4.5 is another strategy to help reduce all-or-nothing statements about writing. On this sheet, you can deconstruct writing into as many minute components as you can, and have the student rate his feelings about each, using three options: "OK," "I don't like it," or "I like it." For example, ask the student, "How do you feel about writing lowercase letters?" and "How do you feel about sharpening your pencil?" It's important to offer many choices that you predict the student will have a neutral or even positive response to, as well as some he doesn't like. After this exercise, students tend to have placed many aspects of writing in the "OK" and "I like it" categories, and few aspects in the "I don't like it" category. The next time the student says, "I hate writing," you can take out this sheet and reframe his statement: "Actually, the chart here says you like writing, but you're still learning how to spell and think of an idea. So, let's review your strategies."

 When introducing this rating activity, start with neutral and preferred items first, and then weave in more challenging components.

 For older students, don't use picture icons in the rating sheet. Use a word bank, or just have the students write in the aspect of writing that they are rating.

Taking Advantage of Technology

The GoodNotes app can take a picture of worksheets and then send the photos to a file hosting service like Dropbox. Now the student can use a worksheet on an electronic device with a stylus. Sometimes, taking the paper out of the equation is helpful. See the section "Writing" in appendix C for more helpful digital ideas.

Creating a Writing Checklist

Using the writing checklist in table 3.5 of *The Behavior Code* as a model, fill out the writing checklist for one of your students. In the left-hand column, list different parts of writing (e.g., spelling, thinking of an idea), including some challenging and some less challenging components, and then add helpful strategies in the middle column. In the right-hand column, the students can note whether they needed the strategy or not.

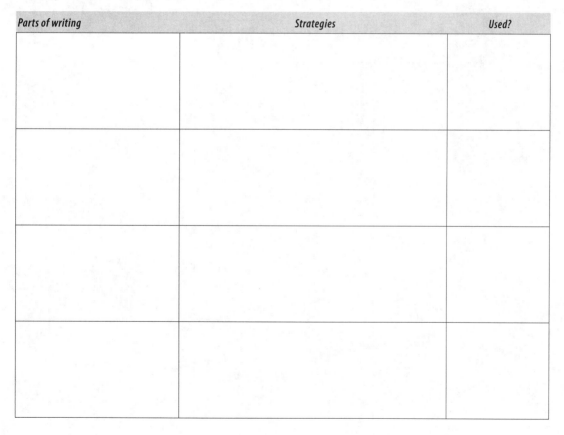

Parts of writing	Strategies	Used?

Creating a "How I Feel About Writing" Sheet

On the "How I feel about writing" form in exhibit 4.5, create a list of the parts of writing for a student to rate (see exhibit 4.6).

EXHIBIT 4.5 **"How I feel about writing"**

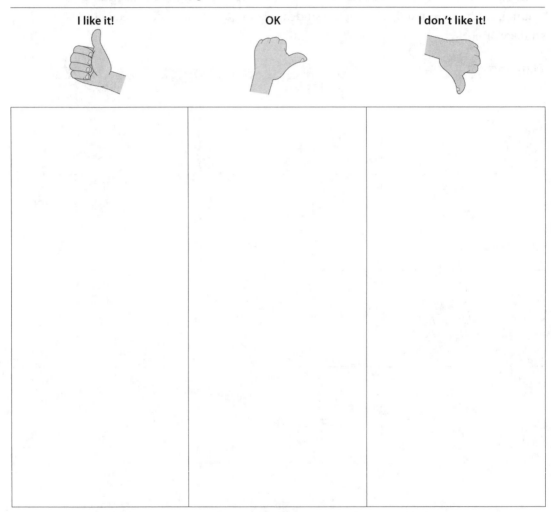

I like it!	OK	I don't like it!

EXHIBIT 4.6   **Parts of writing, sample**

Younger students can cut and paste the parts of writing, shown in the squares below, into the appropriate column of the "How I feel about writing" chart in exhibit 4.5. Older students do not need the picture icons and can merely write the activity in the appropriate column.

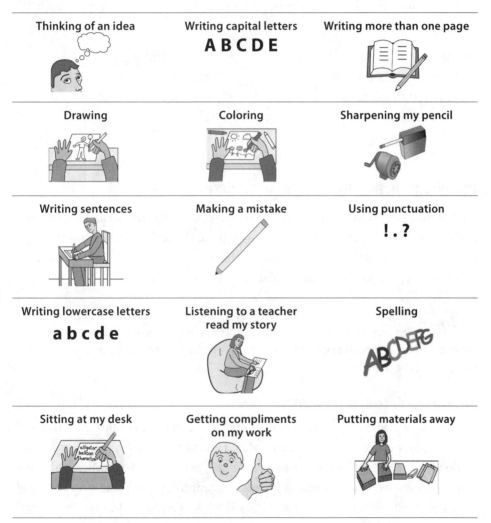

Thinking of an idea	Writing capital letters	Writing more than one page
Drawing	Coloring	Sharpening my pencil
Writing sentences	Making a mistake	Using punctuation
Writing lowercase letters	Listening to a teacher read my story	Spelling
Sitting at my desk	Getting compliments on my work	Putting materials away

Pics for PECS images are used and adapted with permission from Pyramid Educational Consultants, Inc. (www.pecs.com). Pyramid Educational Consultants, Inc., reserves all rights to the Pics for PECS images.

TRAINING IN UNDERDEVELOPED SKILLS: REVIEW

It is essential that the student's FAIR Behavior Intervention Plan highlight explicit strategies for teaching underdeveloped skills. Students can't move forward and change their behavior until these skills are taught.

Skills that may be underdeveloped in students with anxiety include the following:

- Flexible thinking
- Executive functioning
- Frustration tolerance
- Social skills
- Self-advocacy

- Positive thinking
- Motivation
- Self-regulation
- Self-monitoring

TRAINING IN UNDERDEVELOPED SKILLS: EXPANDED

On the following pages, I will describe in more detail the techniques for teaching and accommodating regulation (these are part of the self-regulation accommodation section of FAIR). These techniques include the calming box, body checks, and self-calming practice. I will discuss data collection as well.

Tip *Some students internalize anxiety during the day, but don't show any signs. The parents report that the student doesn't like school and often melts down at home. Self-regulation strategies can help this student avoid building up stress throughout the day.*

Determining Underdeveloped Skills

The only way to formally assess a student's skills is through an evaluation. In school, these evaluations are typically conducted by a school psychologist, but they can also be done out of school by a neuropsychologist, a psychologist, or other evaluators. If the student has had prior testing, it is important to review the testing and speak with the evaluator about the interpretation of the results and how the student's underdeveloped skills may be contributing to his behavior.

Prioritizing Skills and Strategies to Teach

Once a professional has generated a list of a student's underdeveloped skills, it's helpful to work together with your team to prioritize which skill should be focused on first. Generally, *self-regulation* is a priority, because this skill deficit can lead students to escalate to the point of being unsafe, shutting down, or becoming incapacitated. It is also a skill that takes time and practice to learn, particularly for students who have been overcome by anxiety for years and have developed maladaptive coping behaviors. Teaching and reinforcing self-regulation first allows the student to be better prepared to work on other skill areas, although skills such as flexible thinking and positive thinking can be worked on in unison.

REFLECT

Prioritizing Skills and Strategies

Think about a student with anxiety in your classroom, and ask these questions:

1. Has the student been evaluated? If so, what underdeveloped skills were determined?

2. If not, what underdeveloped skills do you suspect are contributing to the student's behavior? Have you asked your team members? Do they agree?

3. Which skills would you prioritize for your student?

4. How are the student's underdeveloped skills being addressed in school currently?

Teaching Self-Regulation

Several strategies and tools, including calming boxes, body checks, and self-calming practice all support students while they learn the skills they need to self-regulate. By collecting data on what works best for each student, we can select the activities that are most effective.

Calming Box

A calming box (as described in chapter 3 of *The Behavior Code*) is an effective way to teach a student to self-calm in times of stress, especially if a separate room is unavailable. Since the calming box is usually used at the student's seat, this approach to teaching self-regulation skills addresses concerns teachers may have about students missing instruction time when on a break. In addition, it provides the student with an anxiety first-aid kit that is always close and available. For this intervention and any others, the students need to be taught explicitly how to use the calming box—to use the items, to think calming thoughts, and to take deep breaths (as opposed to playing with the items, showing them to their peers, chewing on them, etc.). As with all interventions, it is important to collect data to assess the effectiveness of the calming box overall and of each individual item within the box.

For older students (generally fourth and fifth grade and up, though it depends on the student), the calming box looks too babyish. An alternative is to use calming items on a keychain. These can be fidget toys or anything you and the student think may be helpful. One of my students laminated a positive saying from a fortune cookie and put it on her keychain. When she catches herself having negative thoughts, she rubs the paper between her fingers and engages in self-talk with the positive statement to displace the negative thoughts. Another student, who considers himself a tough guy, put a piece of his baby blanket, which he had saved even through multiple foster placements, on his keychain. He rubs it when he is in a conflict situation, to remind him to stay calm and walk away.

Tip   *A photo book of favorite calm places, pictures of the student being calm and peaceful (e.g., asleep on the beach), or photos of comforting relatives can be useful items in a calming box for some students.*

Tales from the Field

Last November, I received an e-mail from Ms. Garcia, a first-grade teacher, telling me that I should visit her classroom to see how well her student, Kendall, was doing. Having heard about the calming-box strategy from a colleague I had consulted with, Ms. Garcia decided to try it with Kendall, who was very oppositional and disruptive in class, calling out and arguing frequently.

When I went to observe the class, Kendall was sitting quietly at her desk during a math lesson. While Ms. Garcia was teaching, Kendall had spilled the contents of her calming box (little dolls, a squeeze ball, and bracelet-making items) on her desk and seemed to be playing with them. After twenty minutes, Ms. Garcia came over and said, "Isn't it great! She stays quiet!"

Later that day, Ms. Garcia and I met to discuss the purpose of the calming box and the importance of teaching Kendall to use it as a tool to calm, rather than a tool to distract her. Together we were able to redefine the calming box with Kendall by reviewing a social story with her and role-playing being upset and using items in the box as tools for self-calming.

Body Checks

Students need to be aware of their dysregulation and emotions before they will ever be able to "catch themselves" and use a strategy independently. They must learn to recognize when they need the regulating strategy. An emotional thermometer (such as the one in table 3.6 in *The Behavior Code*) is a tool to teach and reinforce emotional identification. A student can point to a picture of an emotion and label it. However, the emotional-thermometer chart may not be accessible in all environments, such as the hallway or the gym, and some students have difficulty generalizing the emotional identification skills in these settings. A body check takes emotional identification a step further by teaching the student to identify which physical signs and feelings are associated with their emotion. Learning to read their own body signals is key for students to be able to generalize to other situations the emotional identification skills they learn in school.

When teaching body checks, a teacher can mirror the student's physical posture and facial expressions while explaining, "I notice your shoulders are up, your face is scrunched, and your fists are clenched: you are frustrated right now." Or, "I notice your voice is getting louder and you are moving around a lot in your chair: you are anxious right now." Over time, the student will be able to recognize her own physical cues and identify the accompanying emotions, which is the first step of self-regulation.

Tip *A body check should be introduced and initially taught in private. When teaching the student, start with the prompt, "I notice," which is a neutral way to cue the student. For example, "I notice your folding your arms, and you are not talking, but are just nodding or shaking your head. You are anxious right now." You can even prompt students to notice not only physical but internal cues: "Is your heart racing fast? Are you feeling warm or flushed? You are anxious."*

Rather than overhelping a student to self-regulate by giving him or her directions (e.g., "Sit up," "Lower your voice," or "Stop wiggling"), cue the student to do a body check (e.g., you could whisper, "Kendall, do a body check"). With the same amount of words from the teacher, a reminder to do a body check helps the student to notice his own regulation cues and begin to independently work out a solution, rather than being told what to do. Each body check prompt is a crucial teaching moment where the student learns self-regulation and self-monitoring skills and moves toward independence.

Tip *For older students, you may want to use the term self-check rather than body check, as students become more self-conscious about their bodies and the body-check reminder can evoke uncomfortable giggling.*

Tip *Decide with the student how you will cue or signal a body check. Some students might not mind if you call across the room, but others would prefer if you whisper, write them a note, or use a non-verbal cue.*

Whole-Class Implications

Body checks can be easily implemented for the whole class. Regular self-checks with the entire class normalizes the process and promotes self-regulation and self-monitoring—an essential life skill—for all of your students.

Use a consistent cue (such as saying "self-check" or "body check") when prompting students to monitor their behavior throughout the day. When students hear the prompt, they should recognize and reflect on their behavior in that moment. For example, "Everybody do a self-check. Are you paying attention to your work?" or "Everybody do a self-check. Is your behavior expected and appropriate?" When you prompt them, it's also helpful to have them notice specific behaviors (e.g., paying attention to work). In addition to helping students stay on task and behave appropriately, self-checks also allow students who are accustomed to being called out frequently for inappropriate behavior to notice how often their behavior *is* appropriate.

Tales from the Field

Corday, a first-grader with significant dysregulation due to anxiety, had a very difficult time making the transition from home to school in the morning. Some days, his mother would bring him to school in his pajamas and take him to the nurse so that he could change, because he would refuse at home. Other times, she would put his clothes on over his pajamas in the car in front of the school, and throughout the day, he would complain that he was hot from the layers. Two or three times per week, he would walk into class snapping, yelling, or greeting the teacher with "This is stupid!"

Corday's teacher, Ms. Lee, supported the transition into school by allowing him to start his day with a preferred break to deescalate instead of starting something difficult right away. She also introduced body checks. Corday was resistant to calming activities and would always growl, "I'm ready to work!" even though he obviously wasn't. He needed to learn how to self-regulate, but first he needed to learn to identify his physical signs accurately. I asked Ms. Lee to greet Corday in the hallway in the morning and do a body check. She demonstrated this for him: "I notice your face is scrunched (she mirrored this on her face) and your voice is *loud* (she raised her voice) and your fists and arms are tense. You are frustrated." He looked down and said, "Oh." She encouraged him to enter the room and do a calming activity (a word search), which served as a cognitive distraction, until his body was more calm. He complied for the first time. After a few minutes, she went over and did another body check to mirror and label that his body signs were calm. He responded, "That was some word search!" and rejoined the class. She continued to use body checks throughout the day, and Corday became aware of his body signs. He stopped saying he was ready when he wasn't, and he more accurately identified when he was frustrated.

Self-Calming Instruction and Practice

Students with anxiety will most likely continue to be anxious for months or even years to come. In addition to learning to recognize the physical signs that they are getting anxious, they must learn how to self-calm. Without this crucial coping ability, the students will continue to have difficulty at school and at home.

Many of us have reflexively said, "Calm down" to a student who is crying, unresponsive, or screaming. However, we should never assume that a student is able to calm down.

We often provide safe physical spaces for students to calm down, such as the comfortable calming corners or reading nooks found in many classrooms, calming chairs in a kindergarten or first-grade classroom, or a calm space in the special education teacher or school psychologist's office for older students. These spaces are important, but without also providing the student with instruction in self-calming skills, they aren't effective.

For students who are chronically overwhelmed with anxiety and display it by shutting down or acting out, it is crucial that they practice self-calming in the place they will be when they are upset. I recommend practicing twice a day for two minutes at times when the student is calm. This practice is as important as practicing math facts or any other academic skill that we want students to know automatically. It is helpful to practice self-calming in a specific place designated for that purpose (e.g., the calming chair), because the rehearsal of the skill in this place will help a student react somewhat automatically when he goes there in a moment of panic or heightened anxiety. An adult should practice self-calming with the student initially and then provide a visual list of strategies so that the student can practice independently. The student will then also have access to the visual list when she is upset and actually needs to self-calm. If a designated space is difficult to identify or the student chronically gets upset in various locations, have the student practice her self-calming skills while holding a portable cue (e.g., a small stuffed animal or another object). Once accustomed to holding this object while calming, the student will then be able to translate the skill to the playground, bus, and anywhere else, as long as the student has the object.

Tip   *Post the visual list of strategies near the designated calming space or their seat, so that students can use it as a cue when they are upset. See the sidebar "Taking Advantage of Technology," in this section, for apps that can provide a visual list and cuing systems. Use photographs for younger students or students with low cognitive skills.*

Tip   *Students who show anxiety internally (by putting their head down, ruminating, or having negative or racing thoughts) may not need a separate location in which to calm down. They require a distraction from their own thoughts, which can be done in their seats. A visual list of strategies and self-evaluating sheet can be kept at their desks.*

Tales from the Field

I discovered a self-calming practice with Tilly, a fourth-grade student who became exceptionally irrational and unresponsive when anxious. Our attempts at coaching her to calm in the moment were ineffective; she didn't seem to even hear us. In fact, she typically would keep escalating, screaming and crying until she fell asleep from exhaustion an hour later. I realized she needed to practice repeatedly to internalize this skill. After practicing calming twice per day in the same beanbag chair for a month while she was calm, she became panicked one day and began screaming and crying, and we prompted her to go to the calming beanbag chair. The moment she got in the chair, despite her screaming and irrational statements, she showed automaticity of skills and began to listen to a recorded book independently. Tilly was able to calm herself within ten minutes, which was considered quick for her. When I asked her about it later, she said, "Sitting in the chair reminded me how to calm down."

 Tip *Many students might resist self-calming practice. Have them earn bonus points for practicing.*

Collecting Data

As mentioned in the "Breaks" section in chapter 3, it's important to collect data to determine whether the student is benefiting from the self-calming activity selected. The same data sheet used to evaluate the efficacy of activities for breaks (see exhibit 3.3) can be used to evaluate whether particular self-calming activities are a good choice for your student. In addition to rating the student's physical signs of regulation, make sure to note the student's ability to participate and his receptivity to learning after self-calming (e.g., on-task behavior, class participation).

Self-Rating Sheet for Self-Calming

Gaining independence in coping and self-calming is, of course, our ultimate goal for students with anxiety. We also want them both to learn about themselves and to know what types of strategies are helpful for them. Involving the students in the evaluation of the self-calming techniques is one of the most empowering ways to do this. Have them rate themselves before and after they participate in the self-calming activity (see student's self-rating sheet in exhibits 4.7 and 4.8), and then engage them in a conversation to help them realize what helps them. This self-rating technique can also be used after any break. Teachers can use the data sheet in exhibit 3.3 to decide if a self-calming activity is helpful for the student, in conjunction with the student's using the self-rating sheet in exhibit 4.8.

Tip *For some students, the idea of calming down is hard to understand because it's an abstract concept (especially for students who are young or have low cognitive skills). Using a visual like figure 4.1 may help them comprehend that using a strategy will help them calm down. Add visuals for nonreaders (e.g., a photo of the student making an aggravated expression + picture of the student listening to music = student making a calm expression).*

FIGURE 4.1   **A visual to help students understand the abstract notion of why using a self-calming technique is helpful for a younger student or a student with low cognitive skills.**

Tip *Introduce the self-rating sheet to the student in private. Complete the sheet with her the first time, pointing out the physical signs that you are rating her on.*

Tip *Keep it simple, giving only a few choices—perhaps rating on a scale from 1 to 3. Individualize the rating sheet for each student with specific signs of anxiety that are relevant for him. For older students, cognitive signs like "racing thoughts" or "negative thoughts" can be included as possible signs of anxiety.*

Taking Advantage of Technology

Numerous applications offer helpful tools either for self-calming or to teach the student how to rate himself or herself in these calming techniques. See the following sections in appendix C:

- "Self-Regulation"
- "Video Modeling"
- "Creating Stories to Teach Strategies and Social Skills"
- "Biofeedback"
- "Calming"

If the student has a mobile electronic device available for self-calming or to be included in the calming box, it can be helpful for the student to have access to cognitive distractions such as recorded books. The student could also use a portable CD player or an MP3 player.

PRACTICE

Creating a Visual Self-Regulation Sheet

By yourself or with team members, think of a student with anxiety, and complete the data sheet used to evaluate the efficacy of activities for breaks (see exhibit 3.2), to help you decide which self-calming activities would be appropriate for the student. Once you've completed the data, make a visual list or "menu" of effective self-calming activities for the student.

Now create a self-rating sheet for the student. See the example in exhibits 4.7 and 4.9. Fill in the blank sheet provided in exhibit 4.8. How would you define the three regulation states to be specific to that student. Would you make any other additions or other changes on the sheet?

EXHIBIT 4.7   **Student self-rating data sheet: sample**

Student's definition of their levels of anxiety

1 — Low	*2 — Medium*	*3 — High*
I know this because:	I know this because:	I know this because:
• I am not distracted by my thoughts • I can do my work • My arms are not tense	• I am sometimes distracted by my thoughts • I can only focus on work sometmes • My arms are a little bit tense	• My thoughts are racing or I'm stuck on a thought • I can't get my work done or concentrate • My arms are tense

Date, time, activity	*Before* *What is your worry level right now? (circle one)*	*Strategy* *What activity did you choose?*	*After* *What is your worry level after the strategy? (circle one)*
3/16, 1:15, lunch	1 2 3	Read a book	1 2 3
3/18, 11:15, reading group	1 2 ③	Play with Play-Doh	1 ② 3
3/24, 2:00, spelling	1 ② 3	Play with Play-Doh	1 ② 3
4/1, 11:00, math	1 2 ③	Read a book	① 2 3

EXHIBIT 4.8 **Blank student self-rating sheet**

Student's definition of their levels of anxiety

1 — Low	2 — Medium	3 — High
I know this because: • I am not distracted by my thoughts • I can do my work • My arms are not tense	I know this because: • I am sometimes distracted by my thoughts • I can only focus on work sometmes • My arms are a little bit tense	I know this because: • My thoughts are racing or I'm stuck on a thought • I can't get my work done or concentrate • My arms are tense

Date, time, activity	Before What is your worry level right now? (circle one)	Strategy What activity did you choose?	After What is your worry level after the strategy? (circle one)
	1 2 3		1 2 3
	1 2 3		1 2 3
	1 2 3		1 2 3
	1 2 3		1 2 3

EXHIBIT 4.9   **Student self-rating sheet: sample for younger students**

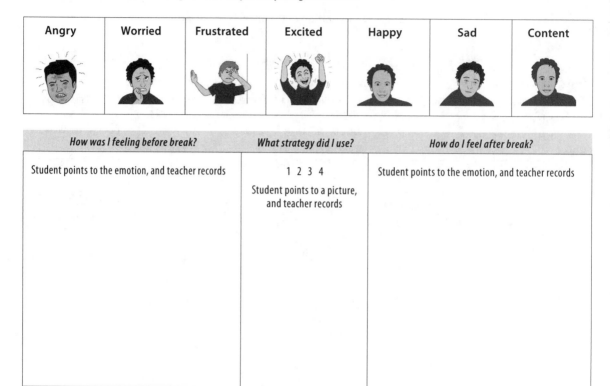

Angry	Worried	Frustrated	Excited	Happy	Sad	Content

How was I feeling before break?	*What strategy did I use?*	*How do I feel after break?*
Student points to the emotion, and teacher records	1 2 3 4 Student points to a picture, and teacher records	Student points to the emotion, and teacher records

Pics for PECS images are used and adapted with permission from Pyramid Educational Consultants, Inc.(www.pecs.com). Pyramid Educational Consultants, Inc., reserves all rights to the Pics for PECS images.

CATCHING IT EARLY: REVIEW

One of the easiest ways to prevent challenging behavior is to catch it early. Subtle, seemingly insignificant changes in behavior, such as a shift from sitting calmly to fidgeting, from talking normally to getting snappy, or from working hard to laying one's head down on the desk, can be signals that a student with anxiety or with oppositional behavior is going to lose control. Teachers who recognize these signals can intervene early with a response that best matches the situation, heading off a meltdown. By checking in with the student, they can determine whether the behavior is due to anxiety or another cause (e.g., hunger, fatigue, the need for the bathroom), and they can prevent escalation.

CATCHING IT EARLY: EXPANDED

Catching students at the first sign of dysregulation is the most effective preventive strategy we have. Each school has educators that are known for being really good with hard-to-reach kids: the paraprofessional we wish we could clone because she can handle anybody, the teacher who really "gets" kids with behavior challenges, or the PE teacher who sends panic through the school when he announces he is retiring. In my experience, their "superpower" is often grounded in an understanding of how to read student's behavior and catch anxiety early with a check-in.

Using the operational definition of anxiety, "any sudden change in behavior," as explained in *The Behavior Code*, can help us understand when we need to be proactive. Once a behavior change is noticed by the teacher, a check-in is appropriate.

 Sometimes, a check-in is not enough and the student needs the teacher to prompt him to use a self-regulation strategy. This may be true if the student's behavior is already more escalated (e.g., arguing or talking back). In these instances, it's best to prompt the student to use a strategy. For example, you could ask, "What strategy are you going to use?" and point to a strategy menu. Or, "Are you going to take a deep breath or use your calming box?"

Verbal Check-Ins

Simply checking in with a student verbally by asking, "How are you?" is a great way to prevent a student from becoming more anxious. When checking in with a student, you might want to rule out some of the student's basic needs. The student might be hungry, tired, or not feeling well. When the student's need becomes clear to you, you can start brainstorming solutions.

Check-in questions are personal. Ask privately, so that peers or other teachers cannot overhear.

Personal questions can be too intimate and uncomfortable for some students, particularly if there is not an established relationship. Indirect questions or comments may be more comfortable. Instead of asking a student if he's hungry (he might be ashamed his parent didn't give him breakfast), you could say, "Here's a granola bar in case you want it." Instead of asking the student if she needs to go to the bathroom, say to the class, "This is a good time to go to the bathroom." An alternative to "Do you need help?" could be "I didn't explain the directions clearly. Let me show you how to start this problem."

Thought Journals

Thought journals are another way for teachers to check in with the student through-out the day. Using a small notebook to write brief notes, the teacher or the student can initiate the correspondence. This private, less noticeable way to communicate can be more comfortable than verbal interaction for some students. A designated place to return the journal on both the desk of the student and the teacher should be established.

Tip *Assure the student that the journal is confidential. It might be best to be per-manently housed in the teacher's desk at the end of every day or when it is not in use. Very personal entries might be removed and stored elsewhere to prevent a peer from reading them. The teacher should also always give the disclaimer that the content of the journal is confidential unless the student discloses worrisome informa-tion: "We will keep this journal private and just between us, unless there is something written in it that makes me worried for your safety or someone else's safety."*

Tip *A thought journal is a great way to process an incident with students. Many times students have difficulty taking responsibility, being accurate, or expressing their feelings about an incident. The thought journal may allow them to do so in a way that is more comfortable and gives them control about when they respond.*

Tip *If a student has writing anxiety and resists this idea, a thought journal is probably not the best intervention for them.*

REFLECT

Planning a Check-In

Think of a student with anxiety in your class, and answer the following questions:

1. Do you have a strong relationship with this student? How do you know?

2. What type of check-in question can you try tomorrow with this student?

3. How will you prevent the check-in from being overheard by peers?

4. Will you ask direct or indirect questions? Why? What are some you will try?

Daily Check-In Sheets

A check-in sheet, completed when the student first enters school, is one way to be consistently preventative with students who are prone to shutting down or acting out. Using this type of sheet makes the teacher aware of the student's level of anxiety at the beginning of the school day and promotes relationship building. It is helpful to ask the student to preview what parts of the school day he is worried about and have him reflect on the strategies he intends to use to cope. When possible, an afternoon check-out is also helpful. At check-out, the student reflects on the day thus far and plans for the next day. Exhibits 4.9 and 4.10 are sample check-in and check-out sheets.

Once the student is frequently using strategies, she can set a goal for the day in the morning and reflect on whether she met her goal in the afternoon. You may want to avoid the goal question with students who have difficulty choosing realistic goals or who get very discouraged when they don't meet a goal.

Tip *Be cautious about asking students how their night was, how they are feeling, or if anything is bothering them. The questions might remind the student of something unpleasant, so when you ask, you must be prepared to give the student a few minutes of your time. Also remember that some students, to stay regulated and more focused on schoolwork, prefer not to reflect on difficulties outside school at all. School can feel safer than home for many students, so you should avoid blurring that boundary.*

Tip *Until the student has memorized or internalized the strategies, you may want to provide a bank or menu of strategies to choose from. This will be especially important for younger students or students with cognitive or language delays. These students will require a menu or bank of strategies either written or represented in picture icons.*

Tip *If writing provokes anxiety for the student, reduce the writing demands in this activity by creating multiple-choice answer options, either in writing or verbally. See also the sections "Self-Regulation" and "Self-Monitoring and Mood Tracking" in appendix C for apps that can be used as a check-in and check-out system.*

REFLECT

Creating Check-In and Check-Out Sheets

Think of a student in your class. After reviewing the sample check-in and check-out sheets (exhibits 4.10, 4.11, and 4.12), answer the following questions:

1. What questions would you include in a check-in sheet for your student?

2. What questions would you avoid? Why?

3. Would you provide a bank of strategies to choose from, or allow the student to come up with them?

4. Would you want the student to label the emotion (e.g., happy, sad, excited) or have the student rate himself or herself on a comfort scale of 1 to 5?

EXHIBIT 4.10   **Sample morning check-in sheet**

Date: _____

1. How are you feeling this morning? (Circle one)

Happy   Sad   Content   Angry   Frustrated   Worried   Excited

2. What is your goal for today?

3. What strategies will you use to achieve this goal?

4. What are you looking forward to today?

5. What do you do you think might be difficult today?
Rate it from 1 to 5, with 1 = easy and 5 = very difficult.

1   2   3   4   5

6. What strategy will you use if you have difficulty?

7. Is there anything you want to talk to a teacher about before you begin your day?

Yes   No

EXHIBIT 4.11   **Sample afternoon checkout sheet**

Date: _____

1. How are you feeling this afternoon? (Circle one)

Sad   Happy   Tired   Calm   Energetic or excited   Angry

2. Did you reach your goal today?

Yes   No

- If you answered no, what can you do differently to reach this goal tomorrow?

- If you answered yes, what did you do to reach your goal? Did you use a strategy?

3. Name one activity or moment that you enjoyed today.

4. What are your plans after school today?

5. Is there anything you want to talk to a teacher about before you leave?

Yes   No

EXHIBIT 4.12   **Sample morning check-in sheet for younger students**

Use this sheet for students in grades K–1 or for low-level readers.

Date: _____

1. How are you feeling this morning? (Have student circle or point.)

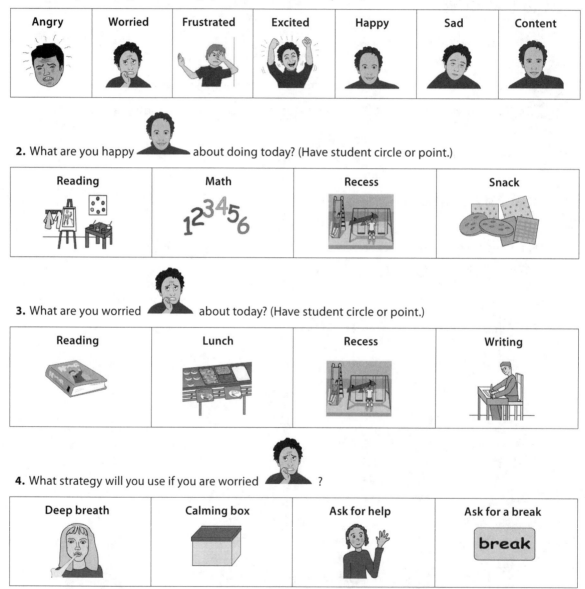

| Angry | Worried | Frustrated | Excited | Happy | Sad | Content |

2. What are you happy _____ about doing today? (Have student circle or point.)

| Reading | Math | Recess | Snack |

3. What are you worried _____ about today? (Have student circle or point.)

| Reading | Lunch | Recess | Writing |

4. What strategy will you use if you are worried _____ ?

| Deep breath | Calming box | Ask for help | Ask for a break |

Catching It Early with Sophia and with Sam

Review the progression of each student's day on the left of the following two charts. With each event, ask yourself the following questions:

1. What are the behavioral signs that the student might be anxious? Underline or circle the signs of the student's anxiety in the description of the event.

2. What is the best response?

3. And finally, could the final incident have been avoided? If so, how?

SOPHIA'S DAY

Event	What is/are the best response/s?
Sophia, a first-grader, entered the classroom and hung up her backpack but kept her coat on, even though the classroom was warm. She sat at her table and started her morning work.	
When Mr. Peters asked the students to pass in their morning work and sit on the rug, Sophia needed four reminders and was the last to sit. She sat on the edge of the rug; this behavior was unusual for her. She did participate when called on.	
During art class, a peer spilled red paint on Sophia's watercolor painting. The teacher told Sophia there was time to make another one, but she snapped at the teacher, saying she would rather just look at a book.	
At recess, Sophia played with two peers, Dahlia and Molly. Sophia had to be reminded several times to stop yelling, and she repeatedly threw the ball over Molly's head and laughed when Molly had to chase it.	
When the teacher announced that it was time to line up, Sophia ran over to the group of kids gathering and threw a ball in Andre's face. Andre began to cry.	

SAM'S DAY

Event	What is/are the best response?
Ms. Chen greeted Sam, a fifth-grader, as he walked into the classroom. Uncharacteristically, Sam walked right by her without a response. He sat down and started to do his morning work.	
When it was time for math, Sam was partners with Kelvin. The boys had to be spoken to for being loud and silly. After about twenty minutes, the teacher had to separate the boys. Sam finished his work independently.	
At snack time, Sam barked at his teacher that he didn't have a snack and he was hungry. She told him he could get crackers from the nurse. He snapped that those were "stale and gross" and went without.	
There was an announcement over the loudspeaker that recess would be indoors today because of the cold temperature. Sam told the teacher he was tired and bored, and he chose to sit at his desk alone during recess.	
Mr. Glasser, the substitute teacher in science class, told the students to pick partners so they could work on the skeleton project. Sam walked out of class without a word.	
When the classroom assistant, Ms. Andrews, followed Sam out, he told her to stop following him. She told him he couldn't leave the class without asking and he needed to return. Sam charged up to her and punched the wall two feet in front of her, saying, "Stop following me! Do you understand English?"	
Ms. Andrews used her cell phone to call the office. When the principal entered the hallway, Sam told her he was just going to the bathroom. The principal invited him into her office to talk.	

RESPONSE STRATEGIES: REVIEW

Preventative antecedent management and teaching underdeveloped skills are the major emphases—*90 percent*—of the FAIR Behavior Intervention Plan for students with anxiety. It's important to shift away from traditional student behavior plans for these students. Rather than giving rewards or points when a student gets through a period without acting inappropriately, use rewards to reinforce the student for using a *strategy*. With this approach, you avoid setting inflexible behavior expectations for a student who has a fluctuating ability to perform.

RESPONSE STRATEGIES: EXPANDED

Decide which strategies you want your students to learn and focus on. I would recommend prioritizing no more than *four* strategies at a time, as more can be difficult to remember and engage in accurately. Self-regulation strategies should be chosen for a student who is chronically overwhelmed by anxiety (i.e., one who displays shutting-down, acting-out, or avoidance behavior). Once the strategies are decided upon, you can provide bonus points for each attempt, practice, or in-the-moment use of the chosen strategies.

Prioritizing Skills to Reinforce

Reinforce whatever skills that you and your team prioritized to teach the student. Self-regulation typically receives the highest priority (if self-regulation is an underdeveloped skill for your student—it may not be), but other skills or strategies may have priority as well.

Whole-Class Implications

Given that close to a third of students will struggle with anxiety at some point in their school careers, shifting our systems to best support this ever-increasing group of students (as well as students with other disabilities) makes sense.[6] Reinforcing the use of self-monitoring and self-regulation strategies is a "universal design" that benefits all students, as these skills are key to success in college and careers.

The whole class can participate in a system of randomly "catching" students using strategies (e.g., "Jenny, give yourself a bonus point for asking for help!"). All older students can have their own self-monitoring sheets to fill out. Younger students can earn bonus bucks or bonus chips that they collect.

Whole-class self-monitoring is a flexible, skill-focused alternative to some of the traditional whole-class point systems or level systems (e.g., the stoplight system, where students remain on the green level until they break a rule and then move to yellow and then red, which usually includes a punishment).

Tales from the Field

A stabilization program for which I was a consultant shifted the emphasis of its traditional point systems from rewarding behavior performance to rewarding the use of strategies and practicing strategies. The word *strategy* became normalized, and every student would earn strategy bucks (which looked like dollars) when he was caught using a strategy. The self-monitoring sheet was given to and used by each student. At the end of every class period, the students would take out their sheets and record the bonus strategy points they accrued as well as reflect on their behavior and if the strategies helped.

Taking Advantage of Technology

Numerous applications are available for helping with behavior reinforcement. For example, the iearnedthat app uses a clever jigsaw-puzzle model to help motivate students to learn and practice a behavioral strategy. You can find this app and others in the section "Behavior and Data Collection" in appendix C. As mentioned earlier, the appendix also lists self-regulation and self-monitoring apps that lend themselves to check-in and check-out systems.

Prioritizing Strategies for Omar

Read the following case studies, and decide which underdeveloped skills the student has and which strategies you will prioritize for the student.

> Omar, a kindergarten student, was adopted from Russia and has been diagnosed with generalized anxiety disorder (GAD). He has had several aggressive incidents over the fall semester, typically when he is playing with other students in the area with wooden blocks in the classroom, but some incidents seem to have no antecedent. Omar has been refusing to do writing workshop, saying it's too boring, and has been resistant to read aloud. The teacher doesn't pair him up with other students during academic times, because he shuts down and puts his head on the table or acts very silly.

1. What are the possible underdeveloped skills underlying the behavior?

2. How would you teach these underdeveloped skills?

3. What strategies would you want the student to work on? Which strategies would you prioritize and have him earn bonus points for using or practicing?

Prioritizing Strategies for Stacey

Stacey is a fifth-grade girl with diagnoses of post-traumatic stress disorder (PTSD) and GAD. Teachers supervise her at recess because she has a history of teasing and pushing peers during that time. During math class, she will scribble on her papers or only produce one problem in an hour. She is described to be overreactive and can start yelling at the slightest change in schedule.

1. What are the possible underdeveloped skills underlying the behavior?

2. How would you teach these underdeveloped skills?

3. What strategies would you want the student to work on? Which strategies would you prioritize and have her earn bonus points for using or practicing?

CHAPTER 5

"You're Not the Boss of Me!"

Strategies and Interventions for Students with Oppositional Behavior

This chapter offers additional information and practice on the critical need to identify warning signs of explosive behavior often seen in students with oppositional behavior. Because a common underdeveloped skill in students with oppositional behavior is the inability to take responsibility for their actions, I offer teachers guidance for processing an incident with students in a way that will promote behavior change.

This chapter also covers many interaction strategies (the *I* component of the FAIR Behavior Intervention Plan) for giving demands and reinforcing positive behavior in students whose oppositional behavior comes from negative-attention-seeking habits, along with strategies for implementing check-in, or self-monitoring, activities with individual students and with a whole class.

CAUSES OF OPPOSITIONAL BEHAVIOR: EXPANDED

Although many students with anxiety or mood disorders may engage in oppositional behavior, often as a result of the fight-or-flight response to anxiety, this section focuses only on disorders that are directly related to oppositional behavior. Additionally, many students who engage in oppositional behavior do not fit any specific diagnostic profile (see exhibit 5.1). For all of these students, however, the same interventions to address the oppositional behavior can be effective.

EXHIBIT 5.1   **DSM-5 update on disorders associated with oppositional behavior**

The *Diagnostic and Statistical Manual of Mental Disorders*, fifth edition (DSM-5) changed how some disorders are categorized. This new edition created a new category called *disruptive, impulse-control, and conduct disorders*, into which oppositional defiant disorder (ODD), conduct disorder (CD), and intermittent explosive disorder (IED) were placed. The criteria for ODD diagnosis also changed, with symptoms now grouped in three types (angry/irritable mood, argumentative/defiant behavior, and vindictiveness), and now include a severity rating. Intermittent explosive disorder has expanded to include verbal and nondestructive/noninjurious aggression, as well as physical aggression. Of note, attention deficit hyperactivity disorder (ADHD), while frequently comorbid with disorders in the disruptive, impulse-control, and conduct disorders category, is listed with neurodevelopmental disorders. The following table gives more detail on the updated diagnostic criteria for these disorders.

SELECTED DISORDERS COMMONLY ASSOCIATED WITH OPPOSITIONAL BEHAVIOR

Disorder	*Features*
Disruptive, impulse-control, and conduct disorders	
Oppositional defiant disorder (ODD)	Consistent, frequent noncompliant and hostile behavior toward authority figures that seriously interferes with ability to function in school and at home. Symptoms are grouped into three types: angry/irritable mood (e.g., loses temper, easily annoyed, angry and resentful); argumentative/defiant behavior (e.g., argues excessively with adults, defies requests, blames others for own mistakes); and vindictiveness (e.g., spitefulness). Can be classified as mild, moderate, or severe, depending on how many settings the symptoms are present in.
Conduct disorder (CD)	Repetitive and persistent pattern of behavior in which the basic rights of others or major age-appropriate societal norms or rules are violated. Symptoms are grouped into four categories: aggression to people and animals (e.g., bullying, weapon use, cruelty to animals); destruction of property (including fire setting), deceitfulness, or theft (e.g., stealing, lying to obtain goods or favors); and serious violations of rules (e.g., running away, truancy). Can be classified as mild, moderate, or severe, depending on the number of problems and the level of their effect on others.
Intermittent explosive disorder (IED)	Failure to control aggressive impulses, resulting in recurrent, frequent, disproportional, impulsive behavioral outbursts (either verbal or physical aggression).
Neurodevelopmental disorders	
Attention deficit disorder (ADD)/attention deficit hyperactivity disorder (ADHD)	Difficulty with attention and organization. Inattentive or impulsive behavior begins before the age of twelve and is seen in at least two settings. Runs in families.

Source: Adapted from Top of Form. American Psychiatric Association, *Diagnostic and Statistical Manual of Mental Disorders: DSM-5*, 5th ed. (Washington, DC: American Psychiatric Association, 2013).

WARNING SIGNS: REVIEW

Most students show warning signs that their inappropriate behavior is escalating before they explode—small behavior changes and other signals that typically precede the student's explosion (e.g., grunting, clenched fists, clenched jaw, using a loud voice when speaking, breathing heavily, rocking back and forth, pacing). When these warning signs appear, it's time to act quickly and remind the student of a regulating strategy.

WARNING SIGNS: EXPANDED

Warning signs should be listed on the top of the student's FAIR Behavior Intervention Plan. To generate a more complete list, team members should brainstorm these warning signs together, as different staff members will have different ideas and experiences with the student.

When a student is showing warning signs, she is more rational and can better access strategies than if the student has had time to stew. For this reason, the warning sign is the last chance to turn the tide before the behavior escalates.

 Sharing the warning signs with students can be a useful way to help them "catch themselves early," as it is a list of concrete behavior clues that the students are escalating.

 When you intervene, remember that the student is upset and may not be able to handle a lot of language and multistep directions.

Deciphering Warning Signs

Read the following scenarios, and make a list of possible warning signs the student is demonstrating.

Scenario 1: Mark

Ms. Shin was passing out math papers to her sixth-grade class when she had to tell Mark to lower his voice, as he was talking loudly to Maria, who was sitting next to him. The class had just finished indoor recess, so the whole room had high energy. Mark rolled his eyes at her and mumbled, but did lower his speaking voice. The teacher attempted to get the class to quiet down and listen to the directions. Mark continued to talk to Maria. Ms. Shin walked over to him and asked him again to lower his voice. Mark looked at her with an intense expression. When she asked if he understood the directions to the math sheet, he did not respond and just continued to stare at her. Ms. Shin told him she would be back and continued to instruct the class. Mark was not engaging in the math lesson and did not have a pencil out. Ms. Shin stopped instruction and told Mark to get a pencil. He stared at her again and grunted, slamming his fist on the desk. Ms. Shin walked over to him and asked if he needed help finding a pencil. Mark snapped back: "I don't need your f—— help, you ugly cow!" and stood up with tense muscles, an intense stare, and heavy breathing. Ms. Shin walked away, hoping he would sit back down.

Warning Signs:

Scenario 2: Cassie

Mr. Forton asked his kindergarten students to line up for music class. Cassie lined up, but the two students next to her were complaining, "Stop! Don't!" Mr. Forton went over to remind Cassie to stop touching people and to keep her hands to herself. Cassie began to bite her sleeve and hop in place while the class continued to line up. Again, Mr. Forton heard a peer complain, so he went over to remind Cassie to keep her hands to herself if she wanted to be on time for music. Cassie yelled, "But I want to go to music!" Mr. Forton reminded her to lower her voice and told her she needed to settle down. He asked the students to start walking, and as the line started to move toward the door, Cassie was looking down, so she didn't start walking. The peer behind her touched her shoulder and said, "Go." Cassie yelled, "Hey!" and shoved him so hard he fell backward.

Warning Signs:

TRAINING IN UNDERDEVELOPED SKILLS: REVIEW

Like students with anxiety, students with oppositional behavior are also attempting to regulate intense feelings. Thus, all of the self-regulation strategies discussed in chapter 3 can also be used with students with oppositional behavior. These students also frequently have trouble taking responsibility for their behavior and accurately assessing their behavior (i.e., self-monitoring). Using a processing sheet such as "Taking Responsibility for Choices" worksheet, in appendix G of *The Behavior Code*, can help students build these skills by showing them how to understand a behavior incident once they are calm.

TRAINING IN UNDERDEVELOPED SKILLS: EXPANDED

In my experience, teachers need practice in helping students with oppositional behavior learn to relay an incident accurately and take responsibility for an action. Attempts to help students learn these underdeveloped skills can feel like a futile struggle. The students may say they are sorry just to appease the teacher, insist that they didn't do anything despite resounding evidence to the contrary, or end up in a standoff with the teacher until the students admit to their error.

Taking Responsibility

Teachers become frustrated when a student won't admit to having made a mistake. "It wasn't me!" "I did not!" We expect students to admit they have erred, show remorse, and then make a reparation (in school, typically in the form of an apology). However, many students are unable to take responsibility, as they cannot accurately process their part in the situation. This inability can be due to a difficulty in processing information when the student is emotionally flooded or stressed.

Processing an Incident

When students are stressed or emotionally flooded in any way, their higher-level brain functioning, including working memory, is affected. Working memory is the ability to keep information in mind—specifically, an event that just occurred or information from long-term memory—and to use this knowledge to regulate behavior, thought, and emotion. Thus, working memory, which is regulated by the prefrontal cortex, includes some of the key skills needed to process an event.[1]

Teachers commonly process an incident with a student right after it occurs (e.g., taking the student into the hallway and asking, "Did you just take Nikhil's iPod?"). But when we ask students to process an incident immediately, we are requiring them to access their working memory at exactly the time when it is most diminished. In fact, in that moment, it is difficult for the student to keep in mind the event that has just occurred, let alone process it or see her own part in it. Some students even experience cognitive distortion, where they recall the incident incorrectly because of the level of anxiety or intensity of emotion they experienced in the moment (e.g., stating that "*everyone* was laughing at me!" when in reality no one laughed). Compounding this anxiety or emotion by confronting them immediately only increases their processing dysfunction, making it less likely they will recall and process the event accurately.

For many students, it is much easier to process the incident when more time has passed and the incident has become less emotionally charged. For some students, namely, those who have not yet mastered the skill of processing, a wait of several days is most beneficial. Until they are able to calm down quickly after an incident and have developed other skills, including flexible thinking and self-regulation, the students cannot be rational and accurate in processing an event immediately. To promote buy-in from the student, have them brainstorm and agree to the most comfortable way for them to process an incident (i.e., with whom, written or verbal).

Tip   *Younger (K–1) students cannot wait as long to process an incident. Try wait-ing a few hours or until the end of the day, depending on the student, but don't wait much longer.*

Tip   *When it's time for the student to process an incident, asking her to write down or record her perspective can be less challenging than asking her to discuss it aloud.*

Tip   *Many students, especially those who have experienced trauma or other life events that included conflict, can become very agitated by being confronted or accused of making a bad decision. Indirect systems of processing an event, such as asking them to write it down or to process it with a familiar and trusted adult who wasn't involved, will more likely help the student to process the incident accurately and even to take responsibility.*

Tales from the Field

Samson Elementary School had a policy stating that if a student had an altercation in class, he would be removed and could return after reflecting on the behavior and apologizing to the teacher. Shae, a fifth-grade student, was spending one to three periods per day in the hallway or the office because of his inability to process incidents, reflect, and apologize.

I met with the team and explained that Shae's trauma history and emotional dysregulation left him unable to process incidents correctly, especially in the moment or shortly afterward. The school agreed that during the next rule-breaking incident, the staff would tell Shae, "We are going to talk about this tomorrow," and not require immediate processing. Later that day, Shae left class to go to the bathroom without asking. The teacher told him, "We are going to talk about this tomorrow," and allowed him to rejoin class. The next day, Shae was asked to process the incident with the guidance counselor (not the teacher, because doing so might have been too emotionally charged for him since he broke her rule). He admitted that he should have asked to go to the bathroom, and he then wrote the teacher an e-mail with this reflection.

Teaching the Skill of Processing

Some students are still not able to process an event correctly, even if we wait to process and have a neutral, safe adult do the processing. We often assume that a student is lying when he denies participation in an incident. Avoid assumptions about the student's ability to remember an event and to see their role in it. Many students have difficulty taking an accurate perspective, a crucial social skill that allows us to understand the thoughts and feelings of others. Perspective-taking ability is even more diminished in these students when working memory is hindered. Without the ability to take another person's perspective, students can't understand the effect of their behavior on others (e.g., Nico asks, "Why is she crying?" after telling Lena he was glad her mom died). Moreover, they may have a distorted memory of events (e.g., a student who says "What? I wasn't even talking to Ying!" after being removed from class for screaming at Ying for several seconds).

Processing an event with the student in an instructional way can help eventually build in the student the necessary skills to process events without support. Drawing out the incident in cartoon form with thought bubbles and speech bubbles can be instructive and skill-building.[2] For example, you could draw a picture of a boy looking concerned while another boy grabs his phone. Tell the student, "When you grabbed Mark's phone, he thought you were taking it not just looking at it!" while writing in Mark's thought bubble, "Oh no! He's taking my phone, or else he would have asked me first!"

Processing Instruction and Sheet Used as a Response

It is often school policy to give a student a consequence for breaking a rule, but consequences don't necessarily change the behavior of a student who is chronically oppositional. Consider instead using a processing sheet or a processing instruction, or both, in response to an incident. This strategy will be infinitely more productive and lead to more positive behavior than would a detention or another consequence.

Tip   *Some school systems, with guidance from specialists, are writing a discipline code statement in the individualized education program (IEP) of students with social emotional disabilities. The statement explains that because of the student's disability, she will be exempt from school's discipline procedures, and it specifies an alternative and parallel response plan.*

Taking Advantage of Technology

Electronic journals can be an indirect way for a student to process an incident. See the section "Writing" in appendix C.

REFLECT

Processing with Your Student

If you have students who are not taking responsibility for their actions, consider the following questions:

1. When you confront the students, do they act defensively? Have you ever assumed they were lying?

2. Are you processing an incident with students shortly after the incident?

3. Will you try any of the strategies listed above? Why or why not?

PRACTICE

Taking Responsibility for Choices Worksheet

With team members or alone, think of a student who has been repeatedly unable to take responsibility for an event. Review the "Taking Responsibility for Choices" worksheet in appendix G of *The Behavior Code*, and decide if you would change or add any questions for this student.

Here are some considerations:

- Is question 3 of the "Taking Responsibility for Choices" worksheet too difficult?

- Does the student have enough perspective-taking skills to answer this?

Would you add any questions? Here are some you might add to the worksheet for the student:

- What did I want?

- What strategy did I use? Was it helpful?

- Was it too difficult to use the strategy?
- Did I forget to use a strategy?
- What adult could I have asked for help?
- Was the activity a good choice for me?

   Would additional reparations, like the following, be better for your student?

- What strategy will I use next time?
- What activity, situation, or space will I avoid next time?
- What activity, situation, or space will be a better choice for me?

STRATEGIES FOR GIVING DEMANDS: REVIEW

Giving demands to a student with oppositional behavior in a way that will promote compliance is an art. Teachers can unintentionally respond in ways that escalate a student's behavior, promote defiance, and counteract a positive teacher-student relationship. Strategies for increasing a positive or compliant response with demands include the following:

- Use a neutral, calm tone (the same intonation you use when you read a bedtime story to a toddler).
- Use "please" in a direction.
- Avoid asking yes-or-no questions.
- Do not turn statements into questions by ending with "OK?"
- Give a choice as often as possible.
- Use declarative language rather than authoritative.
- Give demands in an indirect way, such as writing a note or reminding nearby students of the rules and expectations, rather than directing the statement at the specific student.
- Deliver the direction, and move away.
- Give the student extended time to comply.

STRATEGIES ON GIVING DEMANDS: EXTENDED

Well-meaning educators can make tactical mistakes when giving demands. Thinking through mechanics like respecting student privacy, previewing and giving the rationale for a demand, and providing choices whenever possible can greatly facilitate working with these students. Combining strategies for giving demands can be effective as well. Embedding choice in a nonverbal direction, providing the rationale first and then moving away, or giving a private preview of a demand can be more effective than one strategy alone.

Privacy

Giving demands to a student publicly can set up a dynamic where a student is less likely to comply. Privately giving demands (e.g., a one-on-one conversation in the hall) can be less threatening and easier for a student to tolerate. Whenever possible, writing a note or using a nonverbal signal (e.g., putting a finger to your mouth instead of saying "quiet") provides embedded privacy. Nonverbal interactions are also an almost-foolproof way to avoid a power struggle, as they do not give the student an opportunity to argue.

Tip *You can normalize giving demands via note by giving other students small notes throughout class as well, with positive or negative feedback. For younger students, use pictures rather than words (e.g., a person putting his finger to his mouth to signal quiet).*

Tales from the Field

Adolescents are famous for defying demands. Shellie, a willful sixth-grader, was no exception. Her mother was at her wits end asking her to do chores at home only to ignite a heated argument. I told the mother how nonverbal and written directions paired with giving the student time and space to comply (deliver and move away) would be helpful to avoid such conflicts. I suggested that mom leave the kitchen where Shellie was, go to her own bedroom, close the door, and text Shellie: "Please clean your room." This worked so well the mother started to text Shellie while she was on the bus to school: "When you get home don't forget to take the trash out." The nonverbal direction paired with time and space was very effective in avoiding an argument and increasing the girl's cooperative behavior.

Previewing

It is incredibly helpful to give students time to comply with a demand (e.g., "Can you pick that up before art is over?"), but it's equally important to give them time to prepare for the demand. When students initially hear a direction, their first response is often agitation. Previewing the demand can give them time to calm down after the initial mention. For example, "Joe, next period I'm going to ask you to give Pedro a turn with the calculator—you had a long turn yesterday," or "In a few minutes, I'm going to ask you to put your backpack away."

Rationale

Giving the rationale for the demand before giving the demand is another helpful strategy (e.g., "Oh dear, I don't want anyone to fall! Could you please pick up those pencils?" or "I'm worried that we will run out of glue; please use only a small amount"). Providing the rationale up front ensures that the student *hears* the reason, rather than getting agitated after hearing the direction and tuning out.

Switch Adults

When a teacher gives a demand that the student doesn't like, he might be angry toward her and unlikely to comply. Whenever possible, having a neutral adult (anyone other than the teacher who gave the unpopular demand) follow up with helping the student comply with the direction. The neutral party will be diffusing and likely lead to more cooperative behavior from the student, because the student won't blame the second adult for the unpopular direction and therefore will listen and respond better.

Tips on Giving Demands: Cheat Sheet

- Neutral tone
- Avoid yes-or-no questions
- Choices
- Declarative language
- Indirect
- Deliver, and move
- Extended time to comply
- Use humor when appropriate
- Make it a game
- Give demands privately
- Use nonverbal directions or cues
- Preview the demand
- Provide rationale first
- Switch adults

Taking Advantage of Technology

If the student has access to an electronic device, setting reminders on the device with timers and alarms will allow you to give directions indirectly. For example, have the alarm go off to remind the student to wash her hands before lunch. Since the device, and not the teacher, gives the demand, the student is less likely to get frustrated and more likely to comply. See the apps in the section "Executive Functioning" in appendix C.

Using photographs and previews for recurring demands such as "pack up your backpack" or "write down your homework" electronically can also diffuse a demand and give the student a visual image of the expectation. The image increases understanding (e.g., use Fotobabble to show the student a picture of him writing down his homework with the verbal cue "Remember to write down your homework and get Ms. Lacey to check it"). Now the only direction the teacher has to give is a prompt to look at the picture, or she can just open the picture and have it on his desk.

PRACTICE

Embedding Choice

Review table 4.4 in *The Behavior Code*, and practice restating the direction with a choice for the student.

Restate these directions using each type of choice:

Original direction	Type of choice	Restated with choice
Start your math work.	Where	
Stop talking!	When	
Start your spelling sheet.	Within	
Time to eat snack.	With whom	
It's Ben's turn to roll the dice.	Terminate	
Finish your art project!	Future	
Time to sit on the rug for morning meeting.	Tangible	
Clean up. Recess is over.	Refusal	
Do your math assignment.	Alternative	

Restating Demands

Alone or with your team, restate the direction with each of the demand strategies, and practice aloud, using a neutral tone.

Original direction: "Can you move over and make room for George?"	
Demand strategy	**Restated direction**
Avoid yes-or-no questions	
Choices	
Declarative language	
Indirect	
Deliver, and move	
Extended time to comply	
Give demands privately	
Nonverbal	
Preview the demand	
Provide rationale first	

Original Direction: "Stop calling out, and raise your hand!"	
Demand strategy	**Restated direction**
Avoid yes-or-no questions	
Choices	
Declarative language	
Indirect	
Deliver, and move	
Extended time to comply	
Give demands privately	
Nonverbal	
Preview the demand	
Provide rationale first	

Original direction: "Put the scissors down, please."	
Demand strategy	*Restated direction*
Avoid yes-or-no questions	
Choices	
Declarative language	
Indirect	
Deliver, and move	
Extended time to comply	
Give demands privately	
Nonverbal	
Preview the demand	
Provide rationale first	

POSITIVE REINFORCEMENT: REVIEW

Negative-attention-seeking behavior is any behavior that results in a negative response from an adult or a peer. The behavior is often unintentionally reinforced in school by common practices for addressing undesired behavior (e.g., lecturing, calling the student's name, talking to the principal).

While most students do not seek out or provoke others to get negative attention, those who do may engage in this behavior because of these key aspects of negative attention:

- *Predictability and consistency:* For example, adults respond *every* time a student swears.
- *Efficiency:* Negative attention is faster and perhaps easier to obtain than positive attention.
- *Intensity and drama:* Responses can have a great effect and can be dramatic (e.g., an adult's stopping the car on the highway or a teacher's running after a student).[3]

- *Obvious reaction:* The adult's facial expression, intonation, and voice volume with negative attention is clearer than with positive attention.
- *Verification of a student's poor self-image:* The negative attention mirrors the negative feelings the student harbors about himself or herself.

A combination of positive attention, intermittent reinforcement, and noncontingent reinforcement is the best way to deliver positive reinforcement and eliminate negative-attention-seeking behavior.

GIVING POSITIVE ATTENTION: EXPANDED

Students who seem to prefer negative attention can be difficult for teachers to sympathize with, because the students' behavior appears purposeful and unkind. If we realize that any attention is better than no attention for these students and that negative attention is easier to understand and easier to get than positive attention, we may better understand their behavior. Many of these students have gotten stuck in a learned cycle of acting inappropriately to get attention, which is often inadvertently reinforced in school.

Reinforcing Appropriate Behavior

In school, we often use praise to reinforce positive behavior. Praise is typically delivered quietly and requires a great deal of effort for the student to attain. A student can be appropriately working on a math packet for forty minutes before he gets a "good job" or a check on the top of his paper from the teacher. However, if he swears, the teacher will respond immediately. An imbalance exists whereby negative attention is easier to get, easier to understand, and more potent than positive attention (exhibit 5.2).

Our typical response of praising students just can't compete with the payoff of negative-attention-seeking behavior, so the negative behavior is likely to continue.[4] The community at large also reinforces student's negative behavior—if the student swears in a mall, an airport, or a grocery store, most adults will have a predictable and often obvious reaction.

To minimize negative-attention-seeking behavior and to break a negative interaction pattern between the teacher and the student, you need to make positive

EXHIBIT 5.2   **Benefits of negative-attention-seeking behavior**

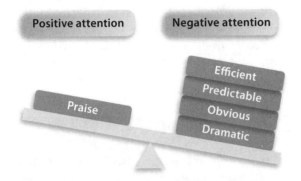

Praise requires hard work on the part of the student and
is unpredictable, subtle, and often low intensity.

attention compete with negative attention in some or all of the domains the student is seeking: predictability, efficiency, obviousness, intensity, and drama. These techniques may only need to be used for a short time to break the negative attention cycle and then can be tapered off until positive attention can be delivered in a less frequent and less intense way.

Becoming More Predictable

Wearing a timer to remind yourself to give the student attention every two minutes is a great way to make positive attention more consistent and predictable. Having the timer visible to the student can make the attention even more predictable. For example, say to the student, "I will be back to see how you are doing in five minutes," and set a timer that remains in view of the student. With this technique, you offer the student an extremely transparent and reassuring way to predict when you will attend to him.

Visual schedules are another way to allow a student to predict the teacher's attention. Putting check-in time on the student's personal visual schedule will allow her to know when the teacher will be attending to her.

Tip   *The frequency with which a teacher needs to give a student positive atten-tion will vary. A student who is entrenched in a negative-attention cycle with the teacher will require positive attention more frequently. As a rule, notice or collect data on how frequently the student is seeking negative attention, and deliver positive attention even more frequently. If the student seems to need constant attention, try a nonverbal signal such as thumbs-up or an OK sign, which will be easier to administer more frequently.*

Tales from the Field

A first-grade student, Tanya, climbed under her desk during science class almost weekly. Ms. Cannon tried everything to get her out. The teacher sat on the floor cajoling Tanya repeatedly, asked her to do special errands, and frequently called on her to participate. These strategies were all giving Tanya attention for sitting under the desk. To turn the tide, Ms. Cannon tried to make herself more predict-able. The next day, when Tanya walked into the room, Ms. Cannon said to her, "I am looking forward to reading with you in five minutes," put the timer on Tanya's desk, and set it for five minutes. When the time had elapsed, Ms. Cannon went over and read the passage to Tanya. The teacher then set the timer for another five minutes and told Tanya she would check the student's work at that time. Tanya did not go under the desk during class—she didn't need to, because she now could predict when Ms. Cannon would give her attention.

Becoming More Efficient

Getting positive attention should be easier and faster than getting negative atten-tion. Teachers tend not to give positive attention for expected behaviors (e.g., stu-dents don't typically get praised for walking into class and sitting as expected). But for a student who is negative-attention-seeking, I recommend celebrating expected behaviors, since for a student with oppositional behavior and underdeveloped skills, demonstrating appropriate and expected behavior is an accomplishment. If a student walks into class and sits down at his seat, take the time to praise. If he raises his hand (especially if this is rare), call on him and thank him for raising his hand, or acknowledge him with a nonverbal thumbs-up if you call on someone else first.

Becoming More Obvious

Many students seeking negative attention do so because the attention is more obvious. For example, our tone of voice and facial expression are exaggerated if we react to a student when we are aggravated. Positive attention is often nonverbal and subdued (e.g., a smile or nod). Using an exaggerated affect and tone of voice when you are giving positive attention can make it more obvious to a student who is not good at reading social cues.

Becoming More Dramatic or Intense

Fortunately, it is rare to have a student who seeks the dramatic aspect of negative attention. Dramatic negative attention can make a student feel powerful—like bolting out of the building with five adults chasing you. For students who do have a pattern of demonstrating behaviors that create a dramatic response, be aware of this and be enthusiastic when cheerleading for an expected behavior.

Tip   *One creative way to help a student get more intense positive attention is to teach the student to tell jokes. Buy a joke book, or download several. The student might find that this is a way to get the intense reaction she wanted, but for something positive!*

Tip   *Be cautious about over-the-top praise with some students, as this causes anxiety. They may worry about setting a high expectation and disappointing you in the future.*

Tales from the Field

Seven years ago, I met a student who helped me see the imbalance between negative and positive attention. Khalil, a fifth-grade boy, was flicking the lights on and off repeatedly throughout the day. It had escalated to the point that the teacher recorded him doing this 244 times in one day. He would walk down the hallway and flick the lights to get a predictable startle response from people in the hallway: "Oh! What happened?" In addition, as he walked by classrooms with open doors, he would put his hand inside the room and flick the lights, and the whole class would laugh, scream, and yell. The light-flicking behavior was eliciting an efficient, predictable, obvious, and dramatic response from staff and students.

I told the staff that we had to make positive attention compete with, and supersede, negative attention. We reinforced Khalil's walking past the light switch without touching it every time. To make the reinforcement predictable, we gave him a token every time he walked past a light switch without flicking it. He thus had a concrete way of predicting the reinforcement. This strategy was more efficient because now he didn't need to raise his hand and flick the switch to get attention. Adding obviousness and intensity to the reinforcement was the biggest challenge. We picked a low-traffic hallway, and the teacher and I walked with Khalil up and down. Every time he walked past the light switch he would get a token and we cheered, using exaggerated facial expressions and tone of voice: "You just walked by the light switch!" After about an hour, we weaned the yelling to a whispered cheer—still keeping the exaggerated affect and tone. After a day and a half, Khalil was only flicking three light switches a day, and the improved behavior continued, even after a week, when the reinforcement was weaned down to his just earning a token and a high five.

Giving Positive Reinforcement

A combination of positive, intermittent, and noncontingent reinforcement is recommended in *The Behavior Code*. The emphasis of the reinforcement should be on skill development and practice, as opposed to behavioral performance. That is, when you are praising a student, emphasize the skill practice, strategy use, or effort: "I love the way you looked at a book while you were waiting—great strategy!" or "I love how you attempted all the problems on this math sheet!" rather than "You got most of these right—great job!"

A common intermittent reinforcement plan is to catch students being good and to use a "caught being good" certificate or token. With some students, you may want to be careful of using the word *good*. This is a judgmental word, as it implies that they can be bad at times. "Caught being flexible" can be a nice alternative for students with oppositional behavior, as flexibility is one of the core skills needed to demonstrate cooperative behavior.

Tip *Some students need to be taught the definition of flexibility. Here is a definition that you may want to use for students: "Stop. Stay calm. Make a new plan." The students should be taught and reminded which strategies will help them stay calm so that they can make the cognitive shift to a new plan.*

Noncontingent Reinforcement

Please review noncontingent reinforcement in *The Behavior Code*—random acts of kindness from a teacher to a student. For example, "Here's a sticker because I like you" or "I know you love baseball, so here's a magazine I brought in for you to look at during quiet reading." Over time, the student will learn the teacher likes him because of who he is, not because of his behavior. Noncontingent reinforcement is one of the most powerful self-esteem-building types of reinforcement. Since students can make behavior mistakes so frequently, you want to make sure that the students don't relate their self-worth to their behavior. The randomly implemented noncontingent reinforcement will allow them to associate the reinforcement with who they are as opposed to how they behaved. Use noncontingent reinforcement often and with any student you are concerned with. Actually, whether or not you are concerned with a student, noncontingent reinforcement helps foster good relationships and self-esteem in all students.

REFLECT

Noncontingent Reinforcement with Your Student

Think of a student of yours who has oppositional behavior. Consider this questions:

1. How often are you using noncontingent reinforcement with your student?
2. Could you be doing more of it?
3. What are the current barriers to delivering this type of reinforcement?
4. What are some possible solutions to these barriers?

Students Who Are Uncomfortable with Positive Attention

As teachers, we constantly use praise and rewards as a means of encouraging and teaching our students. "Good job!" rolls off our tongues throughout the day, and most students are pleased to hear this positive reinforcement. But what do we do when a student rejects—or even sabotages—our praise? Some students will crumple up a paper after being told it was well done, or roll their eyes or make a snarky comment when praised, while others display poor behavior just before they would have earned a prize. For these students, negative attention may feel more comfortable than positive attention. We should see these types of self-sabotage as the student's way of communicating that the current mode of praise and reinforcement makes her uncomfortable, and recognize that a different approach is called for. We don't want to remove positive attention, but we need to change the way we are delivering it.

It's important to discover the underlying cause of the behavior. In some cases, it might stem from self-esteem issues, negative thinking, or both. Another possible—and more serious—reason could be depression. The condition, which encompasses negative thinking and negative self-concept, causes students to feel they don't deserve positive attention. This sentiment makes them reject any attempts at praise. Social anxiety can also be a contributing factor, causing a student to feel uncomfortable with personalized attention or standing out in any way. The underlying cause or causes need to be identified and addressed with support from school mental health personnel ultimately to change the student's behavior.

For students who have a difficult time accepting positive reinforcement, think about which types of praise are prompting the student's unwanted behavior. Public praise—"Nice work, Tyler!"—is a common culprit, especially in the upper elementary and middle-school grades. In these cases, try giving praise privately. But sometimes giving a student positive attention verbally, even privately, is too intimate. We can get around this by writing a note, e-mailing the student, or establishing a nonverbal signal, like a thumbs-up or an OK sign. This will allow the student to receive positive reinforcement in a less intense way. This is also a preferred way to deliver a correction for many students.

> **Tip**   *For a student who is resistant to positive attention, even when it is given in private, use a neutral and calm tone of voice, and be brief.*

The best way to decipher what type of praise or reinforcement a student can accept is simply to pull her aside and ask, "When I want to tell you that you're doing a great job, how should I let you know?" Work together with the student to make a plan that is comfortable for everyone. In addition, putting in the effort over time to build a relationship with the student can make her more receptive to connecting and receiving input.

A Note on Ignoring

Responses such as lecturing the students or having them talk to the principal might be unintentionally reinforcing negative-attention-seeking behavior.

Another response that may not be ideal is ignoring. It's a natural instinct for a teacher to ignore a student who is clearly trying to bait her into an argument or get her to react, but ignoring a student can be ineffective and can even exacerbate the problem. When a teacher ignores a low-level behavior such as a student's sitting under the desk, a student who is focused on gaining the teacher's attention may ramp up the behavior to something that cannot be ignored. For example, the ignored student might start lifting the desk up and banging it down repeatedly or may even escalate to throwing the desk. Making positive attention compete with and supersede negative attention will, hopefully, replace the need for responses such as ignoring in some cases.

Tales from the Field

During one of my first years of teaching, I was a special education teacher in a K–5 building. One of my students, Han, was a fourth-grade boy with diagnoses of generalized anxiety disorder (GAD) and obsessive-compulsive disorder (OCD). Han would occasionally become disruptive when he was upset. He would yell, call the teacher names, and tease other students. One day, Han became so upset he had to leave class and come to my office. When he arrived, he began to swipe objects off my desk and kick the trash can over. I ignored these behaviors as they escalated, until he grabbed a pair of scissors from my desk and I was forced to respond. Three days later, he again became disruptive in class and needed to visit me in my office. He entered the room and went straight toward the pair of scissors. He went immediately to the behavior I could not ignore. I had accidentally reinforced less safe behavior and taught him that dangerous behavior results in attention.

Tip *Another reason ignoring negative behavior from a student is difficult to do in a classroom is that peers don't ignore it. The only person you can control is yourself (so you may be the only person in the room ignoring), and it is very difficult for students to ignore a peer, so the student typically receives attention. Peers will often snicker, look, or even participate or egg on a student by laughing or encouraging.*

Giving Positive Attention

By yourself or with team members, complete the following sheet and reflect on your current use of positive attention and other modes of reinforcement.

Consideration	Current practice	Keep as is	Change now	Change later	Plan for change
Am I giving positive attention twice as often as negative attention?					
What are the nonverbal ways I'm giving positive attention?					
What are the verbal ways I'm giving positive attention?					
Is the way I'm giving positive attention predictable?					
Is the way I'm giving positive attention efficient?					
Is the way I'm giving positive attention obvious and intense?					
Am I worried that my student is uncomfortable with the way I'm giving positive attention?					
Am I using positive reinforcement intermittently or continuously?					

FUNCTIONAL HYPOTHESIS AND ANTECEDENT ANALYSIS: REVIEW

Common antecedents and difficult situations for students with oppositional behavior include the following:

- Peer interactions without adult facilitation
- Unstructured activities (e.g., recess and lunch)
- Interactions with an adult who has an authoritative style or a history of conflict

- Situations when the student is asked to wait
- Times when a teacher places a demand on the student
- Transitions
- Times when the student is told no
- Playing games with peers

In addition, when you are collecting ABC data for these students, look to see if there is a pattern of inappropriate behavior in response to any of the above-listed antecedents or difficult situations. Students with oppositional behavior are often seeking attention, escape, or tangible motivation, so look for these patterns of responses in ABC data.

FUNCTIONAL HYPOTHESIS AND ANTECEDENT ANALYSIS: EXPANDED

One event that is frequently challenging for many students and especially those with oppositional behavior is being told no. No one likes to hear the word *no*, but for some students, the word can result in an intense response. Over time, with support, the student can become desensitized to the word and increase other skills (e.g., frustration tolerance, disappointment tolerance, and flexibility) that led to difficulty with the word. In the meantime, while the student is learning these skills and becoming more able to stay regulated, the teacher may want to accommodate the student and teach him to be aware of this problem.

For a student whose reaction to the word *no* is intense, causing the student to act out or shut down consistently, it may be helpful to teach the student not to ask yes-or-no questions. By asking an adult a yes-or-no question, the student is setting up the interaction to have a 50 percent chance of ending disastrously. A social story or video clip can be used to initially teach the students that yes-or-no questions can be problematic for them. After that, it is important to give the students a replacement behavior. Teach them different ways to ask questions that lead to answers other than no, such as replacing a "Can I . . . ?" question with a "When can I . . . ?" question.

After the student asks a yes-or-no question, cue the student so that she is aware she has used a yes-or-no question and that she needs to use a different question. For example, "Can you ask me in a different way?" or "That was a yes-or-no question.

Can you change the question?" At first, it can help to pair the cue with a sentence starter for the replacement question: "That was a yes-or-no question. You could ask me when can I . . . ?"

 A good prompt for older students is, "Start with a wh—— question," since most wh—— questions will lead to an answer other than no. If this is too hard, give them the sentence starter (e.g., "Where can I . . . ?"), as you don't want to add frustration.

Tales from the Field

Last year, I did several home visits for Ned, a sixth-grade boy with oppositional defiant disorder (ODD) and attention deficit hyperactivity disorder (ADHD). He has a long history of aggressive behavior toward his mother, Kat, and the most explosive incidents occurred when it was just the two of them alone in the house. During one visit, I was in the kitchen coaching Kat as she tried helping Ned do his homework in the living room while she was cooking dinner in the kitchen. We heard something like a growl and a crash come from the living room, and Ned came storming into the kitchen, charging up to Kat and yelling, "You forgot to give me the cookie! Can I have it?!" She looked at me with pleading, frightened eyes. I stepped in front of Ned and said, "You are asking her a yes-or-no question and you can't handle the word *no* That is entrapment." (Ned had just been telling me about spies and entrapment earlier that day.) I said, "You need to change the question. You can ask, 'When can I have a cookie?'" Ned, still angry, snapped, "When can I have the cookie?" and his mother answered, "Right after dinner." He grunted and returned to the living room. Kat used this technique daily after that with all her children. She called it life changing.

Another advantage to teaching the student to avoid yes-or-no questions is that the strategy shifts the focus from what the student can't do to what the student *can* do. The student is now thinking about eating the cookie after dinner rather than not being able to eat it.

 *Especially with younger students, emphasize the word **can** when you respond: "You **can** have a turn on the computer after science class."*

> ## Taking Advantage of Technology
>
> Video modeling can help the student learn and practice appropriate questions. And you can use reminder apps to help the student remember to use alternative questions. See the sections "Video Modeling" and "Executive Functioning" in appendix C.

REFLECT

Your Student Who Can't Handle "No"

Reflect on a student you've had with oppositional behavior and who has difficulty tolerating the word *no*, and answer the following questions:

1. What is the student's current response to hearing the word?

2. What is your plan for this student?

3. How are you going to teach your student that yes-or-no questions aren't working for her?

4. How are you going to prompt the student to ask a different type of question?

5. Are you going to assign bonus points if he takes your cue and asks a replacement question?

SELF-MONITORING: REVIEW

Many students with oppositional behavior have trouble with self-monitoring (i.e., evaluating their own behavior). Luckily, self-monitoring is a skill that can be learned. Using a self-monitoring sheet where both the student and a teacher rate the student's behavior throughout the day can help the student learn to assess his own behavior and to use a strategy when necessary.

SELF-MONITORING: EXPANDED

Self-monitoring is the ability to recognize and keep track of one's own behavior. If you've ever tried to quit smoking or lose weight, you might have been told to keep a log of the number of cigarettes you smoked or the amount food you consumed in a day. These logs, without any other interventions, can be powerful because just being aware of how much you're smoking or eating can change your behavior. Learning to reflect on recent behavior precedes learning to self-monitor in the moment. Once students can monitor themselves in the moment, they can catch themselves before they act inappropriately. These skills are the first steps toward terminating inappropriate behavior altogether.

Regular Individual Check-ins

Developmentally, students learn to reflect on their recent behavior before they learn to catch themselves in the moment. Many students may need a teacher to help them evaluate their behavior throughout the day until they are able to do it themselves. This can be a brief check-in with the student to talk about the student's behavior or a more formal method, such as using a self-monitoring sheet (see exhibits 5.3 and 5.4 for examples). This nonjudgmental conversation is an opportunity to give feedback and help the students learn to evaluate themselves accurately by recognizing behavior that is inappropriate for or disproportionate to the situation (e.g., "Remember how you refused to partner with Kelsey for math buddies?" or "Did you argue with Ms. Gonzales about holding the timer?").

Tip   *To reduce reliance on an adult, students can use an aid like a vibrating timer or a mobile app (see the section "Executive Function" in appendix C for some appropriate reminder apps) to prompt them to do a self-check. This self-sufficiency helps turn a technique into a habit.*

Tip   *The check-ins and teacher ratings on the self-monitoring sheet should never become a power struggle. If the student gets consistently aggravated by this process or anxious by the rating system, skip it and just put a check to record that you had a discussion.*

Tip   *For younger students using the self-monitoring sheet, use picture icons that represent a little bit, a lot, and almost no effort (see exhibit 5.4). Avoid emotion faces and emotion words when they reflect on the student's behavior (e.g., "great job," "OK job," and "bad job") for students of all ages, as this is judgmental and possibly triggering.*

Whole-Class Check-Ins

Regular behavior self-checks with the whole class can normalize the process and teach all students to self-monitor. The practice also allows students who are accustomed to being called out frequently for inappropriate behavior to notice how often their behavior *is* appropriate.

Use a *self-check prompt* to let students know it is time to reflect on their behavior in that moment. It can be general ("Everybody do a self-check and record your behavior") or more specific ("Everybody do a self-check. Are you paying attention to your work?" or "Everybody do a self-check. Is your behavior expected and appropriate?").

Use the easiest method, like a tally or number system, for students to rate themselves on their own self-monitoring sheets at the end of each period. Students can record their behavior on paper or with a mobile device. See the box "Taking Advantage of Technology" below.

> *Tip* *Positive thinking can be a behavior expectation on the self-monitoring sheet (a behavior you want to increase). You may want to determine a concrete way to measure it, such as noting when the student uses a power card, a small card with a reminder of a positive thinking strategy (see chapter 3 of The Behavior Code for more details).*

Taking Advantage of Technology

Apps like Percentally, Repeat Timer, and MotivAider are good self-monitoring tools (see the section "Self-Monitoring and Mood Tracking" in appendix C.

Creating a Self-Monitoring Sheet

With team members or alone, use the template in exhibit 5.3 or 5.4 to create a self-monitoring sheet that is individualized for one of your students. Here are some considerations for creating the self-monitoring sheet:

1. How many strategies have you and your team prioritized for the student? Don't offer the student more than four strategies for earning a bonus point.

2. After every scheduled class period, who will ask the student how her behavior was during the class? How will you do this check-in? In private? Where?

3. Will the student rate herself using the three-point scale described on the sheet in each of the three expected behavior columns? Will you write for the student? Have her write?

4. The teacher will support the student in remembering the details of the class period if needed. Again, where will this conversation happen, and with whom?

5. The teacher will also rate the student's behavior using the three-point scale. Is your student able to handle the rating scale? Do you need an alternative way of filling in that section?

6. How will you discuss with the student any discrepancy between the teacher's rating and the student's?

7. Record one strategy point or bonus point for the use of a strategy written in the strategy box. Will you do this during class, or are you going to wait until after class?

8. At the end of the day, how where and when will you discuss the student's overall day, strategy points earned, and strategies used?

EXHIBIT 5.3   **Self-monitoring sheet**

Name:_____   Date:_____

1	2	3	Strategies:				
Not demonstrated	Somewhat demonstrated	Consistently demonstrated	1. 2. 3. 4.				

	Expected behavior 1		Expected behavior 2		Expected behavior 3		
Schedule	Student	Teacher	Student	Teacher	Student	Teacher	Strategy points
							Total strategy points:

EXHIBIT 5.4 **Self-monitoring sheet for younger students**

Name:_____ Date:_____

1 Almost no effort	2 A little bit of effort	3 A lot of effort	Strategies: 1. Listen to a story 2. Look at a book

Schedule	Use my words		Hands to myself		Listen to directions		Strategy points
	Student	Teacher	Student	Teacher	Student	Teacher	
Morning meeting							
Writing							
Snack							
Recess							
Spelling							
Lunch							
Art							
Math							
							Total strategy points:

Pics for PECS images are used and adapted with permission from Pyramid Educational Consultants, Inc.(www.pecs.com). Pyramid Educational Consultants, Inc., reserves all rights to the Pics for PECS images.

CHAPTER 6

Creating FAIR Behavior Intervention Plans

Now that we have practiced and learned interventions, it's time to put it all together and develop a FAIR Behavior Intervention plan. This chapter discusses considerations for developing FAIR Behavior Intervention Plans, including what to prioritize if you can't do all the interventions at once and whether it's appropriate to mix and match interventions from the different FAIR templates. It also touches on broader uses of FAIR templates in pre-referral meetings and as a guide to whole-class instruction and behavior systems.

At the end of this chapter, I present three case studies of students with either anxiety-related or oppositional behaviors. After reading the case studies, you will analyze the student's existing plan using the concepts from this book and practice choosing and creating a new FAIR Behavior Intervention Plan for each student.

THE FAIR BEHAVIOR INTERVENTION PLAN EXPLAINED: REVIEW

The FAIR Behavior Intervention Plan is different from many behavior intervention plans used in schools today in several important ways. It aims to accomplish the following goals:

- Consider the student's psychological profile and underlying functions of the student's behavior.
- Emphasize preemptive strategies.
- Translate complex knowledge into doable and effective interventions
- Reward students for their ability to use prevention strategies and skills rather than the emphasis being on behavior performance.

- Change inappropriate behavior to appropriate behavior for the long term through skill building rather than simply "managing the behavior."

The acronym FAIR stands for the major parts as well as the major steps required in putting together a FAIR Behavior Intervention Plan:

- *Functional* hypothesis of behavior and antecedent analysis, using ABC (antecedent, behavior, consequence) data and a progress-monitoring data sheet
- *Accommodations*: consideration of accommodations or interventions in the following areas: environment, executive functioning, curriculum, replacement behaviors, underdeveloped skill development, self-regulation, and self-monitoring
- *Interaction* strategies
- *Response* strategies

THE FAIR BEHAVIOR INTERVENTION PLAN: EXPANDED

The FAIR Behavior Intervention Plan *is* a behavior intervention plan. Using the FAIR Behavior Intervention Plan templates in appendixes D and E of this guide, as well as the templates at the end of chapters 5 and 6 in *The Behavior Code*, you will be able to create a behavior intervention plan that will result in long-term behavior change in students with challenging behavior. A FAIR Behavior Intervention Plan is not a supplement to a behavior intervention plan; it *is* a behavior intervention plan.

Using Multiple FAIR Behavior Intervention Plan Templates

Teachers are finding that many students benefit from several strategies—found in several FAIR Behavior Intervention Plan templates—in *The Behavior Code*, because the students' behavior represents more than one type of challenging behavior. The FAIR Behavior Intervention Plan templates are designed for this multifaceted approach, which is greatly encouraged. For example, students with any challenging behavior have some inherent level of anxiety (it's not easy to be a struggling student) so many accommodations from the FAIR Behavior Intervention Plan template for students with anxiety are still helpful for students for whom anxiety may not be the primary concern. Similarly, interacting with a student in a way that promotes compliance and positive responses is universally helpful. For this reason, teachers regularly use both the interaction-strategies section of the oppositional-behavior FAIR Behavior Intervention Plan and the positive-thinking strategies in the withdrawn-behavior FAIR Behavior Intervention Plan.

Incorporating FAIR Behavior Intervention Plans in Individualized Education Plans

Not all students who benefit from FAIR Behavior Intervention Plans have an IEP. For the students who do have IEP services, I have provided sample IEP goals and objectives in appendix A, with language that can be used to reflect the skill-building emphasis in the FAIR Behavior Intervention Plans.

Protocols as a Supplement to FAIR Behavior Intervention Plans

Despite our tireless efforts, crises do arise with students. The best way to ensure the safety of the student and staff in a crisis is a clear, well-practiced protocol of actions. Philosophically, the FAIR Behavior Intervention Plan is a preventative skill-building approach. Because crisis measures are reactive and are not intended to teach a student, but are meant to keep people safe, we may want crisis procedures to be outlined in a separate document. If you have a student who is at risk for bolting, self-harm, making threats, or becoming aggressive or violent, then protocols should be developed. In appendix B, you will find templates for creating safety, bolting, self-harm, and threat protocols.

Implementing a FAIR Behavior Intervention Plan in Stages

After creating a FAIR Behavior Intervention Plan, a teacher might feel overwhelmed trying to implement so many new strategies at once. The team may create the plan and decide to initiate it in stages so that the teacher and the student are not overwhelmed. One way to break the plan into stages is to highlight (in a bright color) the interventions that should be tried first. The first emphasis should always be strategies that support safety. After the teacher is familiar and comfortable with those strategies, the team can highlight more of the document.

Using the FAIR Behavior Intervention Plan Template in Pre-Referral Meetings

Some school systems have been using the FAIR Behavior Intervention Plan templates found at the end of chapters 3, 4, 5, and 6 from *The Behavior Code* to help guide intervention suggestions in pre-referral meetings (student-support team meetings where teachers and other school staff brainstorm support for students who are not on IEPs). Using these templates as a toolkit guides the discussion toward a focus on the student's underdeveloped skills and how to teach and accommodate them. The templates can empower teachers in a brainstorming meeting where the teachers might otherwise be at a loss for helpful ideas.

The FAIR Behavior Intervention Plan and Universal Design

Many of the interventions in *The Behavior Code* have implications for the whole class. Self-monitoring and self-regulation strategies, for example, are integral for success in college and in adulthood, so using some of the suggested strategies in this guide and in *The Behavior Code* modified for the whole class can be beneficial for all students. In several places in this book, I give examples of whole-class implementation of the various strategies in the FAIR Behavior Intervention Plan.

CREATING A FAIR BEHAVIOR INTERVENTION PLAN FOR ATON

The remainder of this chapter will use three examples to give you practice with formulating a FAIR Behavior Intervention Plan. Case studies provide a limited amount of information, but you will be able to discern the student's needs and create a plan. For the first example, follow these steps.

1. Read the case study and complete the first set of questions about Aton's behavior.
2. Read Aton's current behavior plan in exhibit 6.1. Then, analyze his plan by answering the next set of questions. Create a FAIR Behavior Intervention Plan for Aton. Details on exactly how to write up the plan come at the end of each of the three student examples.
3. Later, after reading chapter 7, you can choose which methods you are going to use to assess progress, and create a data collection sheet.
4. Later, after reading chapter 7, you can choose to create a checklist to ensure accurate implementation.

Aton, Grade 3

Aton, a third-grade boy, has diagnoses of oppositional defiant disorder (ODD) and posttraumatic stress disorder (PTSD). He can be oppositional, disruptive, and unsafe. He typically responds to demands by saying no or arguing. On occasion, when the teacher gives Aton a demand, he will laugh out loud and walk out of the room or pace around the perimeter of the room. After trying to persuade Aton to do work repeatedly, the teacher has been resorting to lowering demands, and Aton is allowed to play the computer for several hours each day. Aton often reports that work is too easy or stupid. He hates writing activities and gets a scribe for any assignment requiring any writing. When he does show his knowledge (typically when playing games), he does seem to be on grade level academically, despite his lack of engagement in the curriculum.

His ABC notes suggest that his antecedents and difficult activities are writing, academic demands, unstructured times (lunch and recess), transitions, and public praise. The consequences are one-to-one attention from an adult, negative attention from peers, and successfully avoiding demands or activities. The notes suggest that Mondays and Tuesdays after weekends with his father are significantly more difficult.

He has also been bullying peers on the playground, so the principal has him in the office during recess for the month. Aton's teachers say that sometimes he shows warning signs that he's getting frustrated, but sometimes it comes out of the blue.

Questions About Aton's Behavior

1. Does Aton have anxiety-related, opposition, withdrawn, or sexualized behaviors?
2. What are some antecedents for Aton's undesirable behavior?
3. Does Aton have any underdeveloped skills? Which ones? How do you know?
4. Given the description above, do you think the current behavior plan is working?

EXHIBIT 6.1   **Aton's behavior intervention plan**

DEFINITIONS

- *Oppositional behavior:* ignoring adults, continuing inappropriate behavior when asked to stop (e.g., running in hallway, roaming in halls), making comments under his breath (e.g., "Why? Why?"), using inappropriate language, not completing academic tasks

- *Unsafe behavior:* roaming around building, leaving classroom without permission or without indicating he needs a break, banging on door with his feet, opening and closing outside doors

Here is the current plan for the above behaviors:

1. A calm voice should be used with Aton at all times.

2. If Aton displays oppositional, disruptive, or unsafe behavior, the following actions should take place:

   a. Identify the behavior. For example, "Aton, you are running in the hallway. The expected behavior is that you walk. Please stop."

   b. If Aton does not respond, give him a second opportunity. For example, "Aton, you are running in the hallway. The expected behavior is that you walk. Please stop. I know you can walk; this is your second try."

   c. If Aton does not respond, take away time for undesirable behavior. For every minute that he does not respond, he owes the time in lunch detention (quiet lunch). Since being with peers is motivating, the hope is that he will change his behavior.

   d. When the time comes to owe time, if Aton does not comply, teacher should have him come to the office.

   e. If Aton refuses, his mother should be called and he should be picked up.

Here is the plan for positive behaviors:

1. For positive actions, Aton can earn extra time for desirable activities (e.g., time in the gym, recess, computer).

2. For every fifteen minutes of compliance, Aton should be given two minutes of desirable activity time.

3. For every consecutive hour of compliance, Aton should be given two bonus minutes of desirable activity time.

4. For each time Aton turns his behavior around with one request, Aton can use bonus time at the end of the day.

Questions About Aton's Current Behavior Plan

1. Are the target behaviors measurable? Do the target behaviors identify behaviors that are appropriate and should be increased?

2. Is there a list of antecedents (collected from data) and corresponding interventions to reduce the student's anxiety in those activities or moments?

3. Is the functional hypothesis based on ABC notes or a functional behavior analysis, and is the hypothesis written on the plan?

4. What percentage of the plan is preventative, and what percentage is reactive?

5. Are warning signs listed?
6. Does Aton have underdeveloped skills? Are they listed in the behavior intervention plan?
7. Is the reinforcement system focused on skill building and skill practice?
8. Is there a plan to reinforce, practice, and teach these underdeveloped skills?
9. Are replacement behaviors and strategies taught in this plan?
10. Does this plan use rewards and consequences based on behavior performance?
11. Does this plan list interaction strategies?
12. Given the psychological profile of the student, is this plan going to be helpful? Why, or why not?
13. Given the case study description of the student, which FAIR Behavior Intervention Plan template or templates would you use as your guide?

Putting It All Together: FAIR Behavior Intervention Plan for Aton

Now that you have reviewed the case study and answered the questions thoughtfully, you can now formulate an effective FAIR Behavior Intervention Plan for Aton. Use the FAIR Behavioral Intervention Plan templates in appendix E or F of this guide to make a new plan for Aton. An example of a completed plan for this student is provided in appendix G. Don't worry about filling out the "Data Collection" or "Implementation Checklist" sections near the bottom of the template. These will be discussed in chapter 7.

CREATING A FAIR BEHAVIOR INTERVENTION PLAN FOR DEVAN

Follow these steps to create a FAIR Behavior Intervention Plan for the second student example:

1. Read the case study and complete the first set of questions about Devan's behavior.
2. Read Devan's current behavior plan in exhibit 6.2, then analyze his plan by answering the next set of questions.
3. Create a FAIR Behavior Intervention Plan for Devan.

CASE STUDY

Devan, Grade 6

Devan is a sixth-grade student who has been suspended four times in the first three months of school for aggressive behavior and bolting from the building. He has been diagnosed with PTSD and social communication disorder. Devan has an early life history of trauma; his older brother sexually assaulted him for several years when he was young. His brother was removed from the home but visits on school vacations and holidays.

Devan is extremely bright. He often reports he hates school. Devan hates writing activities and gets a scribe for any assignment requiring more than minimal writing. He also hates when teachers "tell him what to do." Socially, he prefers familiar adults. He has many conflicts with peers and requires supervision at recess and PE.

His ABC notes suggest that his antecedents and difficult activities are writing, pencil-and-paper tasks, demands, unfamiliar adults, unstructured times (recess, lunch), transitions, and social demands. The consequences include successfully escape from demands or nonpreferred activities, and negative attention from adults and peers. Devan has difficulty before, and for days after, long weekends and holidays when he sees his brother.

Devan can have explosive outbursts, including aggression and throwing heavy objects, usually after being corrected or perceiving he has been corrected, although there have been several incidents where the teacher wasn't sure of the reason.

Questions About Devan's Behavior

1. Does Devan have anxiety-related, opposition, withdrawn, or sexualized behaviors?
2. What are some antecedents for Devan's undesirable behavior?
3. Does Devan have any underdeveloped skills? Which ones? How do you know?
4. Given the description above, do you think the current behavior plan is working? Why, or why not?

EXHIBIT 6.2 **Devan's behavior support plan**

PROACTIVE STRATEGIES TO CONTROL ANTECEDENTS AND TEACH FLEXIBILITY

- Set up Devan's schedule before he arrives at school so he knows what is expected throughout the day.
- Point out when Devan uses flexible social skills. For example:
  - "Today in math you were listening nicely with eye contact. Nice job."
  - "Thanks for being flexible with changing your seat!"
- A quiet or private distraction-free space should be provided outside of the space where Devan does his academic work. This space should be for taking quiet breaks, to process any altercations, and to have private conversations.

BEHAVIOR SUPPORT PLAN

- Teachers will give concrete feedback almost immediately after positive or negative behaviors by processing the incident with him in his quiet space.
- Devan earns checks, which are recorded on a point sheet and tallied after each class period. Checks are awarded every five minutes if Devan is:
  - Following directions
  - Being safe
  - Participating
- After four checks, Devan is permitted a five-minute break.
- If Devan earns eight checks in a class period, he is allowed a "fun break."
- Fun breaks consist of quiet, fun activities that Devan chooses (e.g., working on a model, art, a board game, computer time).
- If Devan doesn't earn enough checks for a fun break, because of negative behavior, he may still have a break, but it should be a quiet time with no games.

Questions About Devan's Current Behavior Plan

1. Are the target behaviors measurable? Do the target behaviors identify behaviors that are appropriate and should be increased?
2. Is there a list of antecedents (collected from data) and corresponding interventions to reduce the student's anxiety in those activities or moments?
3. Is the functional hypothesis based on ABC notes or a functional behavior analysis, and is the hypothesis written on the plan?
4. What percentage of the plan is preventative, and what percentage is reactive?
5. Are warning signs listed?

6. Does Devan have underdeveloped skills? Are they listed in the behavior intervention plan?

7. Is the reinforcement system focused on skill building and skill practice?

8. Is there a plan to reinforce, practice, and teach these underdeveloped skills?

9. Are replacement behaviors and strategies taught in this plan?

10. Does this plan use rewards and consequences based on behavior performance?

11. Does this plan list interaction strategies?

12. Given the psychological profile of the student, is this plan going to be helpful? Why, or why not?

13. Given the case study description of the student, which FAIR Behavioral Intervention Plan template or templates would you use as your guide?

Putting It All Together: FAIR Behavior Intervention Plan for Devan

Use the FAIR Behavior Intervention Plan templates in appendix E or F of this guide to make a new plan for Devan. Don't worry about filling out the "Data Collection" or "Implementation Checklist" sections near the bottom of the template. These will be discussed in chapter 7.

CREATING A FAIR BEHAVIOR INTERVENTION PLAN FOR ANGELA

Now you are ready to create a FAIR Behavior Intervention Plan for the last student example. As before, follow these steps:

1. Read the case study and complete the first set of questions about Angela's behavior.

2. Read Angela's current behavior plan in exhibit 6.3, and then analyze her plan by answering the next set of questions.

3. Create a new FAIR Behavior Intervention Plan for Angela.

Angela, Grade K

Angela, a six-year-old with a diagnosis of GAD and OCD, did very well making the transition to kindergarten. She had almost no difficulties until right before Thanksgiving, when the teacher noticed that her previously infrequent requests to go to the nurse were becoming daily occurrences during academics (mostly during reading and writing). Angela also started to refuse to go to recess and music, saying the kids were too loud.

Angela's parents reported all year that she was crying on the way to school, saying she hated it, and she didn't enter school until around 10:00 or 11:00 a.m. twice in November, because of her mother's difficulty getting her out of the car to enter the building.

The ABC notes suggest that Angela's antecedents and difficult activities are transitions (to school, and within the school day), writing, reading, social demands, recess, lunch, music, unfamiliar adults, times when her favorite peer interacts with others, times when the teacher leaves the room, and public praise. The consequences typically include one-to-one attention from an adult or a peer and avoidance of work or nonpreferred activities. Angela has more difficulty coming to school after a long weekend or a vacation or if she has been out sick (she always misses more than one day for an illness).

In December, Angela began refusing recess daily. When coaxed into going outside, she began to hide in the play structure or the surrounding trees. She started to cry and whine at most academic tasks, especially writing, and when asked to read, she often repeated that she was stupid and hid in the cubbies. She became very clingy to one girl in particular and even hit a boy who was conversing with Angela's peer, telling him, "She doesn't like you." Angela needs constant reminders to keep appropriate personal space with that girl and others and to stop touching (often hugging peers and holding their hands). The teacher refers to Angela as her shadow, as Angela follows her around the class and even down the hall if the teacher needs to do an errand. But when the teacher gives Angela a compliment or enthusiastic praise, Angela becomes sullen.

Questions About Angela's Behavior

1. Does Angela have anxiety-related, opposition, withdrawn, or sexualized behaviors?
2. What are some antecedents for Angela's undesirable behavior?
3. Does Angela have any underdeveloped skills? Which ones? How do you know?
4. Given the description above, do you think the current behavior plan is working? Why?

EXHIBIT 6.3 **Angela's Behavior Intervention Plan**

TARGET BEHAVIORS

- Compliance when asked to go to recess
- Increasing awareness of personal space

PREVENTATIVE MEASURES

- Angela will have preferred seating in front of, or next to, the teacher.
- The teacher will preview the visual schedule of the day with Angela, highlighting any change such as indoor recess or a substitute teacher in art class.
- Angela will be reminded that she can only go to the nurse once per day, and only if she is really feeling sick.
- The first thing in the morning, Angela will choose from the prize box a reward to work toward. The reward will be placed visibly on the teacher's desk to motivate Angela.
- The teacher will review the break strategy with Angela every morning.

RECESS COMPLIANCE PROCEDURE

Student behavior	Teacher behavior
In the morning, Angela will review with the teacher the rules about going to recess.	Teacher will remind her that she is earning the previously selected prize.
If Angela goes to recess . . .	Teacher will give her a token.
If Angela earns five tokens . . .	Teacher will give her a prize.
If Angela doesn't earn a token one day . . .	Teacher will remind her she can try the next day.

RESPONSES TO PERSONAL SPACE INFRACTIONS

Student behavior	Teacher behavior
If Angela engages in touching others . . .	She will be reminded that she is earning the previously selected prize and will be given a warning.
If Angela stops touching the peer . . .	Teacher will give her a token.
If Angela continues to engage in touching others . . .	Teacher will separate her from the peer.
If Angela earns five tokens . . .	Teacher will give her a prize.

REPLACEMENT BEHAVIORS TAUGHT

- *Breaks:* Angela will be reminded of her break plan in the morning.
- *The replacement behavior:* Angela will be reminded that she can raise her hand and ask for a break when she feels anxious or frustrated, instead of running to the cubbies and hiding.

Questions About Angela's Current Behavior Plan

1. Are the target behaviors measurable? Do the target behaviors identify behaviors that are appropriate and should be increased?
2. Is there a list of antecedents (collected from data) and corresponding interventions to reduce the student's anxiety in those activities or moments?
3. Is the functional hypothesis based on ABC notes or a functional behavior analysis, and is the hypothesis written on the plan?
4. What percentage of the plan is preventative, and what percentage is reactive?
5. Are warning signs listed?
6. Does Angela have underdeveloped skills? Are they listed in the behavior intervention plan?
7. Is the reinforcement system focused on skill building and skill practice?
8. Is there a plan to reinforce, practice, and teach these underdeveloped skills?
9. Are replacement behaviors taught in this plan? If so, is the replacement behavior chosen adequate?
10. Does this plan use rewards and consequences based on behavior performance?
11. Does this plan list interaction strategies?

12. Given the psychological profile of the student, is this plan going to be helpful? Why, or why not?
13. Given the case study description of the student, which FAIR Behavior Intervention Plan template or templates would you use as your guide?

Putting It All Together: FAIR Behavior Intervention Plan for Angela

Use the FAIR Behavior Intervention Plan templates in appendix D or E of this guide to make a new plan for Angela. Don't worry about filling out the "Data Collection" or "Implementation Checklist" sections near the bottom of the template. These will be discussed in chapter 7.

CHAPTER 7

Tools for Monitoring Progress and Implementation

The previous chapters were designed to help you practice choosing interventions for students with anxiety-related or oppositional behaviors, creating FAIR Behavior Intervention Plans, and teaching explicit skills to help these students improve their behavior.

But how do you know that the plans that you have designed are helping?

In this chapter, we will take the FAIR process two steps further. The best way to know whether a student is improving is to compare data taken before and after the intervention is implemented. To assist educators in collecting this type of data, I introduce two ways to gauge student progress.

However, one more step is needed. Even after we carefully create FAIR Behavior Intervention Plans for each student according to her needs, if we do not then follow through and ensure that the plan is used consistently and correctly, we don't know whether to attribute any changes in behavior (for better or worse) to the plan.[1] We can't link the outcome to the treatment. Two checklists will also be introduced to help educators implement interventions with fidelity (accurately and consistently). Only in this way can we provide effective interventions for students with challenging behavior.

MONITORING PROGRESS

Students change frequently, as do other variables that affect their behavior (e.g., pop quiz in science, substitute teacher in Art class). Collecting and analyzing data daily, weekly, and monthly is crucial to helping students with complex profiles. Both *The*

Behavior Code and this guide stress the importance of recording ABC (antecedent, behavior, and consequences) data prior to choosing interventions. However, in addition to ABC notes, progress monitoring data is useful for determining whether the interventions you've chosen for your student are, in fact, working. A data sheet for monitoring the student's progress from her (before intervention is tried) combines ABC data with progress-monitoring data (exhibit 7.1). The sheet can be used not only to discover behavior patterns and to hypothesize function, but also to measure student progress toward appropriate behavior. Using this sheet alone or in combination with the participation and compliance data sheet (exhibit 7.2), you obtain a full picture of how your chosen accommodations, interactions, and responses are working.

To collect baseline data (vital for assessing later progress), these data sheets should be completed before interventions or behavior intervention plans are implemented. You should then collect data regularly throughout the school year on an ongoing basis to monitor progress to see if the frequency of the behavior has improved and to note and plan for any changes in antecedents. Tweaking the data sheets, deciding on the duration of baseline data collection, and implementing more complicated data systems to determine students' progress should be done in consultation with behavior analysts, school psychologists, special educators, or social workers who are behaviorally trained. Data helps us know if the interventions we are using with students are helping and if the student is making progress. Let us look at the data sheets in detail.

Establishing a Baseline, and Monitoring Progress

The data sheet in exhibit 7.1 focuses on frequency—the number of times the behavior occurs during an activity—and ABC data. ABC data can be collected for some or all of the target behaviors on any given day. ABC data is especially helpful if a behavior is new or especially concerning (unsafe) or if it has changed or isn't improving. Consult your team specialist in the beginning about how long to collect this data and what behaviors to choose.

Assessing Participation and Compliance

Exhibit 7.2 can be used to measure progress or lack thereof in participation, compliance, and unsafe or challenging behavior and provides additional information about the student's classroom functioning.[2] This data sheet will allow professionals to measure increases or decreases in participation in class, which is a different measure of progress than behavior frequency. Measurable definitions of target behaviors should be included on the back of the sheet for easy reference.

Measuring Behavior

In most cases, the frequency of incidents of targeted behaviors is the most useful measure of progress (i.e., a decrease in incidents of inappropriate behavior). However, there are other ways to record and measure behavior. The sample data sheets can be adapted, or you can design alternative data sheets to collect data on other dimensions. Here are various ways behavior can be measured:[3]

- *Frequency:* How often a behavior occurs during a period of observation. Frequency is the most common form of behavior measurement.
- *Rate:* How often a behavior occurs during a specific period (e.g., head-banging incidents per hour)—calculated by dividing frequency by time. This is used to measure if the behavior is slowing down typically—it's a different, more specific way of representing frequency.
- *Duration:* How long an incidence of a behavior lasts. Measuring duration allows us to see if behavior incidents are reducing in length (whether or not the frequency of the incidents has changed). Shorter durations may indicate that the student is learning to calm himself and or is becoming less upset about each incident.
- *Latency:* The length of time between a stimulus and a response. Latency represents how long the student takes to comply with a demand or to initiate work.
- *Accuracy:* The percentage of behaviors that are performed accurately. For example, a student might answer 90 percent of math problems (e.g., nine out of ten) correctly, or a student raises her hand quietly 80 percent of the time (i.e., of the ten times she raises her hand, she does it quietly eight times; the other two times, she calls out).
- *Permanent product:* Tangible items that result from a behavior (e.g., completed worksheets and other class work). Student work can be an excellent measure of on-task behavior, participation, and comprehension.

- *Intensity:* The vigor with which a behavior is performed. Intensity is commonly assessed for students with explosive behavior, such as aggression. Sometimes, the frequency of a behavior does not change, but the intensity does. Measuring intensity allows us to see improvement. For example, a student who previously punched a teacher with full strength is now pushing with minimal contact and minimal force. You would create a numerical intensity scale (e.g., from 1 to 5) to use as a measure.

- *Topography or shape:* The behavior can change topography (the way behavior appears). Ultimately, we want to see students shape their behavior toward more appropriate conduct. Instead of crying and yelling about how hard work is, the student is now putting his head down quietly. This behavior is still concerning, but shows improvement as it is less stigmatizing and makes the student stand out less.

Tip   *Collecting data on the behavior we want to increase (the replacement behavior or appropriate behavior) is a good focus for the FAIR Behavior Intervention Plan and subsequent data sheets, as the increase in appropriate behavior is what we want to ultimately achieve.*

Taking Advantage of Technology

See the section "Behavior and Data Collection" in appendix C for ideas on collecting data electronically. Videotaping behavior incidents is a great way to record topography and to measure improvement by comparing baseline video data and with videos after behavior interventions have been implemented.

Creating Data Sheets for Your Student

1. Alone or with your team, think of a student for whom you will be writing or have already written a FAIR Behavior Intervention Plan. Which behaviors are you going to collect data on? Behaviors you want to decrease (problem behavior) or those you want to increase (replacement behaviors and appropriate behaviors)?

2. If there are many replacement behaviors needed, which behaviors are you going to prioritize?

3. Which strategies are you going to prioritize? Why?

4. How might you use data sheets to measure whether your interventions are working?

5. Are there any barriers to completing these data sheets? What are some possible solutions?

EXHIBIT 7.1   Baseline and progress monitoring data sheet

Date, day of week: _____

Time	Staff	Activity	Target behavior 1:	Target behavior 2:	Target behavior 3:	Strategy 1:	Strategy 2:	Strategy 3:
8:30–9:00								
9:00–9:30								
9:30–10:00								
10:00–10:30								
10:30–11:00								
11:00–11:30								
11:30–12:00								
12:00–12:30								
12:30–1:00								
1:00–1:30								
1:30–2:00								
2:00–2:30								
2:30–3:00								

ABC DATA FOR A TARGET BEHAVIOR

Please record any instance of _____ below in ABC format.

Setting events	Activity, time	Antecedent	Behavior	Frequency, duration, intensity[a]	Consequence

Source: Adapted from Sidney W. Bijou, Robert F. Peterson, and Marion H. Ault, "A Method to Integrate Descriptive and Experimental Field Studies at the Level of Data and Empirical Concepts," *Journal of Applied Behavior Analysis* 1, no. 2 (1968); Beth Sulzer-Azaroff and G. Roy Mayer, *Applying Behavior-Analysis Procedures with Children and Youth* (New York: Holt, Rinehart and Winston, 1977).
[a] Latency, rate, and accuracy may be added to this column, depending on the type of behavior being measured.

EXHIBIT 7.2   **Participation and compliance data sheet**

Student: _____   Time start: _____   Time end: _____

Teacher observed: _____   Activity observed: _____

Minutes	Student was *functionally participating in activity?*[a] (Record *yes* if participating for entire interval with less than 10 sec. off-task)	Student *complied with all directives* during the interval? (Record *yes* if all directives followed within 10 seconds of each directive)	Student engaged in unsafe *behavior* during interval? (Record *yes* if behavior occurs during any part of interval)	Student engaged in *challenging behavior during the interval?* (Record *yes* if behavior occurs during any part of the interval)
1	Yes / No	Yes / No	Yes / No	Yes / No
2	Yes / No	Yes / No	Yes / No	Yes / No
3	Yes / No	Yes / No	Yes / No	Yes / No
4	Yes / No	Yes / No	Yes / No	Yes / No
5	Yes / No	Yes / No	Yes / No	Yes / No
6	Yes / No	Yes / No	Yes / No	Yes / No
7	Yes / No	Yes / No	Yes / No	Yes / No
8	Yes / No	Yes / No	Yes / No	Yes / No
9	Yes / No	Yes / No	Yes / No	Yes / No
10	Yes / No	Yes / No	Yes / No	Yes / No
11	Yes / No	Yes / No	Yes / No	Yes / No
12	Yes / No	Yes / No	Yes / No	Yes / No
13	Yes / No	Yes / No	Yes / No	Yes / No
14	Yes / No	Yes / No	Yes / No	Yes / No
15	Yes / No	Yes / No	Yes / No	Yes / No
16	Yes / No	Yes / No	Yes / No	Yes / No
17	Yes / No	Yes / No	Yes / No	Yes / No
18	Yes / No	Yes / No	Yes / No	Yes / No
19	Yes / No	Yes / No	Yes / No	Yes / No
20	Yes / No	Yes / No	Yes / No	Yes / No

[a] Fill out the following chart to specify the behaviors whose definitions are measurable.

MEASURABLE DEFINITIONS OF BEHAVIOR

Measureable definitions should be filled in below for easy reference. If more room is needed this section should be copied on the back of the preceding participation and compliance data sheet.

Unsafe behaviors	
Challenging behaviors	
Functional participation	
Compliance with directives	

EVALUATING IMPLEMENTATION WITH CHECKLISTS

Treatment integrity (also known as treatment fidelity) has been defined as the degree to which an intervention or a treatment is implemented as planned in a comprehensive, consistent way.[4] In the school context, we often call it teacher integrity, and it refers to whether the curriculum and interventions prescribed for a student are used consistently and accurately as intended so we can assess if the intervention is helpful.[5]

Teacher integrity can be concretely measured with a checklist of actions that are essential to the intervention. You can use this list to see what percentage of these actions was completed accurately.[6]

Schools are busy places. It is difficult to find time to apply interventions, assess student gains, and use data to guide instruction. It is particularly hard to evaluate ourselves and assess the treatment integrity of our own plans. Enlisting colleagues as resources for evaluating the adequate implementation of plans and interventions can be a useful and supportive way to collaborate and advance your practice and ultimately improve student outcomes.[7] Open, nonjudgmental collaboration can prevent educators from inconsistent or inaccurate implementation. Collaboration also helps educators from falling into old patterns of responding to behavior or forgetting parts of the intervention.

Implementation Checklist: For Overall or Specific Intervention

Implementation checklists can assess implementation fidelity on two levels: for the entire FAIR Behavior Intervention Plan or for individual interventions. Examples of both types of checklists, adapted with permission from Dr. Katherine Terras, are shown in the following pages. Ideally used daily or weekly, the checklists can be used for self-evaluation, or some teachers may use them as part of an observation (i.e., a colleague or supervisor completes the checklist to give you feedback).

Assessing fidelity is particularly helpful when you are first learning an intervention, because the assessment helps you ensure that the intervention is implemented accurately. The assessment should be conducted again, after you have been doing the intervention for several weeks, because people tend to drift and need to refresh themselves on the details of their actions.

Sample Checklists for Nelli's FAIR Behavior Intervention Plan

Exhibit 7.3 shows the completed FAIR Behavior Intervention Plan used with Nelli, a student described in chapter 3 of *The Behavior Code*. Exhibit 7.4 is an implementation checklist for Nelli's FAIR Behavior Intervention Plan as a whole. Exhibit 7.5 is an implementation checklist for a single intervention (breaks) for Nelli. Analyzing these samples will give you a quick idea of how an implementation checklist can be created. Note that target ratings should always be 4 because we want to aspire for consistency and accurate implementation, even though it is challenging, so the student will learn faster and achieve optimal progress.

Sample Checklist for Joe, a Student Without a FAIR Behavior Intervention Plan

Many accommodations and interventions embedded in each FAIR Behavior Intervention Plan can be multistep and challenging to implement. Therefore, you may wish to create one implementation checklist for one intervention at a time, to help ensure the accuracy of implementation of any accommodation or intervention you are concerned with.

These single-intervention checklists are also useful for teachers of students who don't require a whole FAIR Behavior Intervention Plan. A sample of single-intervention checklist for Joe, a student who needs help with writing, is provided in exhibit 7.6.

All implementation checklists, like those in these samples, should include an *analysis of implementation sheet* (included at the end of exhibits 7.4–7.9) so that teachers can reflect on their ability to implement strategies, seek help if needed, or make another plan such as changing the intervention if it is too difficult to implement.

EXHIBIT 7.3   **FAIR Behavior Intervention Plan for Nelli**

Student's Name: ___Nelli_____   Date: __2/14/2014_____

TARGETED BEHAVIORS (be as explicit as possible):

Asking for help: any instance of Nelli's asking a teacher for help, either asking
   verbally with the word *help* or pointing to an "I need help" card

Using designated break space: any instance of Nelli's leaving a designated space
   and arriving at one of three designated break spaces within five seconds of her
   leaving the designated space

F   Functional Hypothesis

Document all instances of targeted behaviors, using ABC data sheet
(minimum of ten incidents)

List antecedents and difficult activities from ABC data or observation to be
addressed in this plan:
* Transitions
* Unstructured times

Hypothesize the function of behavior (circle one or more):
* Escape

List any pattern of consequences, using the ABC data:
* Removed from the classroom
* Peers removed from class removed
* Teacher does not persist with demand

List any setting events of note:
* Mother's boyfriend moved out
* Change in medication

A Accommodations

Environmental

☑ Schedule regular breaks

☑ Arrange alternative lunch

Executive functioning

☑ Use timer

☑ Use visual schedules

☑ Preview nonpreferred tasks in the morning

Curriculum

☑ How-to-draw cards available

☑ Other technology support: spell checker

Teaching underdeveloped skills

☑ Social skills

☑ Flexible thinking

☑ Self-regulation

☑ Executive functioning

(All will be taught by social worker twice per week)

Replacement behavior

☑ Social worker will teach Nelli, and have her practice, how to ask for a break appropriately; teacher will prompt in the classroom

Self-regulation and self-monitoring

☑ Have student use regulation scale (e.g., emotional thermometer)

☑ Prompt for body-check cues throughout the day

☑ Encourage daily self-calming practice in or out of the classroom with yoga

☑ Have student develop and use calming box

☑ Have student use self-regulation chart: "what to do when I feel . . ."

☑ Schedule breaks—noncontingent escape to prevent avoidance behavior (before whole-class lessons for five to ten minutes)

I Interaction Strategies

- ☑ Teacher will respond to any sudden change in behavior with supportive response
- ☑ Use noncontingent reinforcement: bring in pictures and magazines about fairies
- ☑ Use leadership-building and self-esteem-building activities: Nelli can act as PE helper for kindergarteners once per week
- ☑ Work on explicit relationship building: when teacher can, she will eat lunch with Nelli occasionally and play basketball with her, one on one, in the gym

R Response Strategies

- ☑ Prompt Nelli to use a strategy when she shows signs of anxiety
- ☑ Nelli earns bonus points when she demonstrates a self-regulation skill, including using her calming box, practicing self-calming, taking a break (yoga), or doing a body check when prompted

EXHIBIT 7.4   Implementation checklist for Nelli's FAIR Behavior Intervention Plan

Teacher: Ms. Tucker

Date: 3/3/2014

School: Washington Elementary School

Evaluator (self or other): Self-evaluation

Student: Nelli

Intervention: FAIR Behavior Intervention Plan

	0 Never 0%	1 Almost never 1–25%	2 Sometimes 26–50%	3 Almost always 51–75%	4 Always 76–100%	Target rating
Accommodations						
Three scheduled breaks given daily	0	1	2	3	4	4
Alternative lunch arranged and implemented daily with two or more typical peers (facilitator embeds social skills vocabulary when appropriate)	0	1	2	3	4	4
Visual schedule reviewed every morning, and nonpreferred work reviewed and started, one to one with teacher	0	1	2	3	4	4
Timer used for nonpreferred tasks	0	1	2	3	4	4
Writing accommodations provided before a writing task: how-to-draw cards, spell checker	0	1	2	3	4	4
Have Nelli label emotions intermittently throughout day by having her point to the emotional thermometer, or ask her to point when she is asked, "How are you feeling?"; corresponding strategies prompted as well	0	1	2	3	4	4
Prompt Nelli to do a body check when she shows signs of anxiety or dysregulation	0	1	2	3	4	4
Facilitate or assign an adult to facilitate daily self-calming practice where Nelli practices yoga	0	1	2	3	4	4
Calming box available and near Nelli's desk at all times. Prompt Nelli to use it when she shows signs of anxiety or when asked to do something difficult	0	1	2	3	4	4
Prompt Nelli to take a break noncontingently to maintain regulation	0	1	2	3	4	4

	0 Never 0%	1 Almost never 1–25%	2 Sometimes 26–50%	3 Almost always 51–75%	4 Always 76–100%	Target rating
Explicit instruction: Social worker sees Nelli twice per week to work on explicit instruction of social skills, flexible thinking, and the replacement behavior of asking for a break	0	1	2	3	4	4
Interaction strategies						
Notice and respond to any sudden change in behavior with a check-in	0	1	2	3	4	4
Use noncontingent reinforcement at least once daily: e.g., bring in pictures of fairies for her to look at	0	1	2	3	4	4
Concrete relationship-building and leadership activities once per week	0	1	2	3	4	4
Responses						
When Nelli shows signs of anxiety or dys-regulation, prompt her to use a strategy	0	1	2	3	4	4
Award Nelli bonus points at end of every period when she demonstrates a self-regulation skill or practices another skill	0	1	2	3	4	4
Data						
Data collected as intended	0	1	2	3	4	4

ANALYSIS OF IMPLEMENTATION

Teacher: Evaluator (if not self):

Date:

1. Are all interventions at the target rating for adequate fidelity? If not, which ones don't meet the target?

2. For each intervention *not at target*, what is the plan?

Intervention	Action plan

EXHIBIT 7.5 **Implementation checklist for single intervention: breaks for Nelli**

Teacher: Ms. Tucker
Date: 3/3/2014
School: Washington Elementary School

Evaluator (self or other): teacher observation of
Ms. Tucker by Mr. Long

Student: Nelli
Intervention: Breaks

Steps for implementing breaks	0 Never 0%	1 Almost never 1–25%	2 Sometimes 26–50%	3 Almost always 51–75%	4 Always 76–100%	Target rating
Collect data on Nelli's regulation state before she goes on a break.	0	1	2	3	4	4
Prompt Nelli to fill out a self-evaluation on how she feels before the break.	0	1	2	3	4	4
Preview activity for the break and the termination cue (e.g., timer, what time it is over) when the break is finished.	0	1	2	3	4	4
Monitor Nelli's implementation of break.	0	1	2	3	4	4
Collect data on student's regulation state after student returns from break.	0	1	2	3	4	4
Prompt to fill out a self-evaluation on how she feels after break.	0	1	2	3	4	4
Teacher and student decide if break was helpful and if another intervention is necessary.	0	1	2	3	4	4
Review data weekly to determine if changes need to be made in break activities, break procedures, or when breaks are used.	0	1	2	3	4	4

ANALYSIS OF IMPLEMENTATION

Teacher: Evaluator (if not self):
Date:

1. Are all interventions at the target rating for adequate fidelity? If not, which ones don't meet the target?

2. For each intervention *not at target*, what is the plan?

Intervention	Action plan

EXHIBIT 7.6 **Implementation checklist for single intervention: writing checklist for Joe**

Teacher: Mr. Long
Date: 3/3/2014
School: Washington Elementary School

Evaluator (self or other): *teacher observation of Mr. Long by Ms. Tucker*

Student: Joe
Intervention: Writing checklist

Steps for implementing writing checklist strategy	0 Never 0%	1 Almost never 1–25%	2 Sometimes 26–50%	3 Almost always 51–75%	4 Always 76–100%	Target rating
For at least a week before using the writing strategies checklist, record data on any inappropriate behaviors Joe might be demonstrating during writing, how much writing was produced in a given class, and any language student used to describe writing.	0	1	2	3	4	4
Preview with Joe yesterday's writing checklist. Point out what strategies student used.	0	1	2	3	4	4
Prompt Joe to get started with writing assignment after directions are given and student relays that directions are clear.	0	1	2	3	4	4
If student does not get started quickly or stops working at any point, teacher will offer assistance.	0	1	2	3	4	4
After writing assignment, go over writing checklist with student (e.g., "I noticed you used this strategy and that strategy"). Check strategies used.	0	1	2	3	4	4
Collect data daily on any inappropriate behaviors student might be demonstrating during writing, how much writing was produced in a given class, and any language the student used to describe writing.	0	1	2	3	4	4
Review data weekly to determine if changes need to be made in strategies offered and to determine if student is making progress.	0	1	2	3	4	4

ANALYSIS OF IMPLEMENTATION

Teacher: Evaluator (if not self):

Date:

1. Are all interventions at the target rating for adequate fidelity? If not, which ones don't meet the target?

2. For each intervention *not at target*, what is the plan?

Intervention	Action plan

Making an Implementation Checklist

1. Review the FAIR Behavior Intervention Plan that you developed with your team.

2. Write the steps and interventions from the FAIR Behavior Intervention Plan into the corresponding categories on a FAIR Behavior Intervention Plan implementation checklist (a blank form is provided in exhibit 7.7).

3. Complete the checklist yourself, or ask a colleague to observe you.

4. Complete an analysis of implementation (a blank form is provided at the end of exhibit 7.7), including an action plan for any interventions that are not at the target rating of 4.

5. Continue to use this checklist weekly to assess your implementation of the interventions.

6. Now choose one intervention to focus on.

7. Write the steps of the intervention into the corresponding categories on an intervention implementation checklist (a blank form is provided in exhibit 7.8).

8. Complete the checklist yourself, or ask a colleague to observe you.

9. Complete an analysis of implementation (a blank form is provided at the end of exhibit 7.8), and create an action plan for any interventions that are not at the target rating of 4.

10. Continue to use this checklist weekly to assess your implementation of the specific intervention.

PRACTICE

Putting It All Together

Now look back at the FAIR Behavior Intervention Plans you created for Aton, Devan, and Angela in chapter 6. Complete the sections for "Data Collection" and "Implementation Checklist" so that you would be able to monitor the students' progress toward appropriate behavior and to ensure that you, as their teacher, would be implementing the interventions with fidelity.

EXHIBIT 7.7   **Implementation checklist for the FAIR Behavior Intervention Plan**

Teacher: Evaluator (self or other):
Date: Student:
School: Intervention: FAIR Behavior Intervention Plan

	0 Never 0%	1 Almost never 1–25%	2 Sometimes 26–50%	3 Almost always 51–75%	4 Always 76–100%	Target rating
Accommodations						
	0	1	2	3	4	4
	0	1	2	3	4	4
	0	1	2	3	4	4
	0	1	2	3	4	4
	0	1	2	3	4	4
	0	1	2	3	4	4
	0	1	2	3	4	4
	0	1	2	3	4	4
	0	1	2	3	4	4
	0	1	2	3	4	4
	0	1	2	3	4	4

	0 Never 0%	1 Almost never 1–25%	2 Sometimes 26–50%	3 Almost always 51–75%	4 Always 76–100%	Target rating
Interaction strategies						
	0	1	2	3	4	4
	0	1	2	3	4	4
	0	1	2	3	4	4
Responses						
	0	1	2	3	4	4
	0	1	2	3	4	4

ANALYSIS OF IMPLEMENTATION

Teacher: Evaluator (if not self):

Date:

1. Are all interventions at the target rating for adequate fidelity? If not, which ones don't meet the target?

2. For each intervention *not at target*, what is the plan?

Intervention	Action plan

EXHIBIT 7.8　**Implementation checklist for specific interventions**

Teacher:　　　　　　　　　　　　　　　Evaluator (self or other):
Date:　　　　　　　　　　　　　　　　Student:
School:　　　　　　　　　　　　　　　Intervention:　FAIR Behavior Intervention Plan

	0 Never 0%	1 Almost never 1–25%	2 Sometimes 26–50%	3 Almost always 51–75%	4 Always 76–100%	Target rating
Steps for implementing						
	0	1	2	3	4	4
	0	1	2	3	4	4
	0	1	2	3	4	4
	0	1	2	3	4	4
	0	1	2	3	4	4
	0	1	2	3	4	4
	0	1	2	3	4	4
	0	1	2	3	4	4

ANALYSIS OF IMPLEMENTATION

Teacher:　　　　　　　　　　　　　　　Evaluator (if not self):
Date:

1. Are all interventions at the target rating for adequate fidelity? If not, which ones don't meet the target?

2. For each intervention *not at target*, what is the plan?

Intervention	Action plan

Individualized Education Program Goals and Objectives

INCORPORATING SKILL BUILDING INTO THE INDIVIDUALIZED EDUCATION PROGRAM

Individualized education programs (IEPs) traditionally use behavior goals and objectives that delineate expected behavior progress (e.g., "Timmy will reduce screaming by 50 percent of baseline levels"). Supplementing these behavior goals and objectives with separate skill-building goals and objectives allows the IEP team to formally focus on and monitor the student's progress in these skills through progress reports and annual reviews. Here are some examples of IEP goals and objectives that represent the skill building that is the focus of your FAIR Behavior Intervention Plans into the IEP.

Goal: Self-Regulation

Kamari will use a strategy such as a calming box or asking for a break when showing visible signs of stress in nine out of ten opportunities, with 70–100 percent accuracy.

Objective: Self-Regulation

Across two settings and with two adults, Franco will use his calming box when showing visible warning signs of stress in nine out of ten opportunities, with 100 percent accuracy.

During math class, Torgan will ask for a break, choose an appropriate break strategy, and return to the math activity in nine out of ten opportunities, with 70 percent independence.

Goal: Replacement Behaviors

Kevin will use functional communication such as using his words or asking for help to express frustration in eight out of ten opportunities, with 70 percent independence.

Objective: Replacement Behaviors

Across two school settings and with two adults, after functional communication practice, Porsha will express her frustration or dislike appropriately when she is given a nonpreferred direction in eight out of ten opportunities, with 70 percent independence.

During writing or spelling activities, Chung will appropriately communicate frustration by using his words and asking for help, independently in eight out of ten opportunities, with 70 percent accuracy.

Across two school settings and with two adults, SueMai will extinguish explosive incidents and replace them with functional communication (e.g., "I need help") independently and with 100 percent accuracy and with 70 percent independence.

Goal: Emotional Identification

Leticia will identify distressing situations and triggers in seven out of ten opportunities and with 90 percent accuracy.

Objectives: Emotional Identification

Harriet will learn to identify stressful situations or triggers, thoughts, and behaviors that contribute to her emotional distress, with adult support, in seven out of ten opportunities and with 90 percent accuracy.

Goals: Writing

Demitri will be able to label his emotional state, use a self-calming strategy, and increase his time on-task and compliance with writing in eight out of ten opportunities with 70 percent independence.

Objectives: Writing

Paul will be able to label his emotional state verbally (e.g., "I'm frustrated") and will implement self-calming strategies (e.g., taking deep breaths or saying "oh well") independently in nine out of ten opportunities with 80 percent accuracy.

After she is given a writing checklist, Cora will increase her stamina for writing tasks by ten minutes in nine out of ten opportunities each semester, with 90 percent independence.

Given accommodations, Marcia will comply with teacher directions or activities involving writing and spelling skills in eight out of ten opportunities with 70 percent independence and 90 percent accuracy.

Goals: Transitions

Given transition support, Trudy will stop a preferred activity and shift to a nonpreferred activity in nine out of ten opportunities with 80 percent accuracy.

Objectives: Transitions

Across school settings and staff, Maria, given transition support, will comply with teacher directions to stop a preferred activity (e.g., playing on the computer, playing at recess) in nine out of ten opportunities with 80 percent accuracy.

Given transition warnings and support, Nathan will demonstrate increased flexibility in situations where he needs to shift from a plan or schedule he preferred to a less preferred plan or schedule in eight out of ten opportunities with 80 percent independence.

Protocols: Safety, Bolting, Threat, and Self-Harm

Review the sample protocols for safety, bolting, threat, and self-harm, and together with trained school personnel, tailor them to fit the specifics of your school and staff.

The best way to keep a student in crisis safe is to have a planned and organized staff response. In many districts I've consulted for, I've created protocols that outline appropriate procedures to the four most common crisis situations:

- *Safety:* student displays aggressive behavior.
- *Threat:* student makes a verbal, nonverbal, or gestural threat to harm another person.
- *Self-harm:* student makes a verbal, nonverbal, or gestural threat to harm himself or herself or to commit suicide.
- *Bolting:* student leaves the designated area or building.

There are several advantages to providing protocols for staff. Protocols alleviate the need for staff with varied training to solve problems under stress. Additionally, protocols establish procedures to follow in different crisis situations; outline effective communication between staff, parents, and emergency responders; and provide a guideline for training and practice so that staff members are ready when they need to be.

Tip *Crisis protocols should be separate supplementary documents to the FAIR Behavior Intervention Plan. The behavior intervention plan is, philosophically, a teaching document, while crisis procedures are not a means of teaching students but rather a necessary way to keep them safe.*

CONSISTENCY

Without the use of these protocols, well-meaning staff members are required to determine how to react in a stressful moment—a time when their problem-solving ability could be diminished because of intense stress and the speed with which these events unfold. This hasty decision-making can lead to an overreaction (e.g., calling 911 when a kindergarten student threatens a peer) or underreaction (i.e., underestimating the severity of the incident, such as allowing the student who made a self-harm attempt to walk home alone after school or not reporting a student's suicidal statement). The varied backgrounds that school adults bring to these situations mean that two adults may respond very differently to the same situation.

Having protocols allows school staff to respond consistently and appropriately to incidents. Protocols spell out the set of student behaviors that are of concern and help the staff understand the severity of the incident and respond properly and consistently.

COMMUNICATION

The quick responses required in crisis situations can result in miscommunication. This problem is more likely when we go without a planned communication system, such as carrying walkie-talkies or cell phones. Consider these plausible examples:

- When a student bolts, a principal may send one teacher to run around the building looking for the student when another staff member has the student safely inside.
- In a moment of concern, a teacher calls 911, but the social worker thought the teacher called the parent, so the parents were not called.

Protocols should detail the communication system to be used in a crisis, and should be *signed* by the parent or guardian (as proof of receipt of the document) so that staff members know they are proceeding with parents' prior knowledge of protocols and parents will not be surprised. Getting parents' input on how they want to be contacted, how much information they prefer to be left on voicemail, and whether they want the student's emergency contacts to be called if the parents cannot be reached is important and helpful.

TRAINING AND PRACTICE

All too often, the protocols are reviewed in September, but not are needed until months later, by which time staff members might have forgotten the details. Protocols should be reviewed and practiced often to build an automatic, appropriate, and consistent response when it is needed. One way I've promoted ongoing familiarity is to keep the protocols in a binder and have relevant staff members initial that they've reviewed the protocols monthly. Keeping the binder close at hand (e.g., in a red binder on the teacher's desk) also allows staff to find the protocols easily in a stressful moment.

For students who are aggressive, it is important to have at least four staff members per building certified by a nonviolent crisis training program that specializes in the safe management of students with aggressive behavior.[1] Only these staff members should physically contact the student, and only as a last resort.

Sample crisis protocols are provided on the following pages in this appendix.[2] Only trained school personnel should create and tailor these protocols for the individual school and student, because many variables need to be considered to ensure the safety of students and staff and because every possible variable cannot be covered in any single guide. Legal advice and input from other departments such as fire and police may be advisable when schools are first establishing these protocols. The protocols should be developed realistically considering the resources available at the school. Some schools have access to a mental health outreach agency and have a full-time mental health clinician like a school psychologist in the building. In contrast, some schools have only minimal mental health support and no access to mental health agencies and will need to wait for a neighboring school to send over a school psychologist during a crisis. Especially for these latter schools, the protocols should thus include how to deal with a student in crisis until resources available to the school are contacted and arrive if they are not on the premises already. Once protocols are created, schools need to provide adequate training for all staff.[3]

WHOLE-CLASS PROCESSING

We never want to normalize a crisis witnessed by students, but neither do we want to assume it was not upsetting to witness. Processing the incident with the class is important. See the chapter 7, "Commonly Asked Questions," of *The Behavior Code* for suggestions on how to do this.

SAFETY PROTOCOL

Unsafe behavior
Unsafe behavior for the student is defined as: *Example definition:* any behavior that could cause a student serious injury to himself or herself or another person. Behavior includes but is not limited to hitting, bolting, punching, kicking, biting, choking, throwing objects at a person, and any physical contact with another person that could cause harm.

Preparatory steps to be put in place

- Staff (including the classroom teacher) will have [walkie-talkies or working cell phones] on them at all times.
  - *Tip:* If cell phones are to be used for emergency situations, staff members should have updated phone numbers available at all times and should ensure that their phones work in all parts of school property.
  - *Tip:* If walkie-talkies are to be used for emergency situations, staff members should ensure that the devises work in all parts of school property and check batteries daily.
- *At least four* staff members certified by a crisis prevention program will be on the premises at all times.
- Classroom teacher keeps a copy of this protocol [state where]
  _____.
  - *Tip:* Protocol should be kept in a consistent, easily accessible place in the classroom.
- Principal, secretary, and [other relevant parties] also have copies of this protocol.
- The crisis leader is: _____.
- Other crisis team members are:
  - _____
  - _____
  - _____
- Crisis team members will spend at least fifteen minutes a week building a positive relationship with the at-risk students, as unfamiliar adults will likely add to the student's distress in a crisis.
- The crisis leader will be notified immediately via [cell phone, walkie-talkie, a page by secretary] if there is an incident and the leader is in the building.

- If the crisis leader is absent, the secretary will notify an alternate member of the team that he or she is the substitute crisis leader and will notify the teacher who the substitute crisis leader is that day.
- Every incident is documented.
- This protocol will be reviewed weekly by all staff working with an at-risk student to ensure correct implementation.

If a student exhibits unsafe behavior

1. Student will have a FAIR Behavior Intervention Plan (see attached) [attach the student's FAIR Behavior Intervention Plan to this protocol document] that will be followed daily.

2. If the crisis leader deems the situation safe, he or she will check in with the student and determine if the student can remain in the room and what de-escalation techniques (e.g., take a break, use a strategy) would be helpful and implement them.

3. If the crisis leader deems that the student can stay in the room, the leader will assist the student in using a calming technique, engage the student in communicating his or her feelings, wants, or concerns, and, if appropriate, assist the student in reengaging in the activity.

4. If the crisis leader deems the situation unsafe, he or she will ask the teacher to remove the class to the designated area: _____ [playground, library, cafeteria, etc.], and wait for the crisis leader to inform the teacher if it is safe for the class to return. The crisis leader will then follow the steps outlined below, under "Student Deemed Unsafe."

5. If student exhibits any unsafe behavior despite implementation of the FAIR Behavior Intervention Plan and de-escalation techniques, the classroom teacher or another staff member should _____ [call the office and request the assistance of the crisis team, or call the crisis leader by walkie-talkie or phone]. The _____ [office or crisis leader] will notify other members of the crisis team.

Student deemed unsafe
If the student behaves in a way that will cause himself or others serious or imminent harm, one or more trained crisis team members may be required to intervene physically
[Outline protocol for unsafe behavior here in accordance with a nationally certified crisis prevention program] *Physical intervention or seclusion will be used as a last resort.*

Return to the classroom
If the student needed to leave the classroom, he or she will remain out of the classroom or activity until the student is able to show evidence of calm, cooperative behavior. Calm, cooperative behavior is defined as:
Example definition: the student is able to follow simple directions and answer simple questions. The crisis leader will accompany the student back to the classroom and remain in the room for several minutes until the student is deemed able to remain in the classroom with the teacher.

Parent/guardian notification
The student's parent or guardian will be called by the staff on the same day that the behavior incident occurred. The crisis leader or designee will contact the parent or guardian. If staff doesn't reach the parent or guardian personally, the staff will leave a voicemail and try to contact the parent or guardian again within the school day.

Documentation
Any staff involved with or witness to the behavior incident will fill out incident forms (or restraint/seclusion forms if necessary) on the same day the incident occurred. Copies will be sent to parent or guardian and administration.

Emergency protocol

If student exhibits unsafe behavior in the following ways, the emergency protocol will be initiated:
 	
1. Staff will follow this safety protocol
2. Staff will call student's parent or guardian ***and*** will call:
   • _____ [911 or mental health emergency service agency]
   • Parent phone number: _____
   • Mental health emergency service agency phone number: _____
3. If staff doesn't reach the parent or guardian personally, staff will leave a message while another staff member calls 911 or mental health emergency service agency. If parent has previously agreed, contact the sequence of emergency contact numbers provided by the parent or guardian after calling 911 or mental health emergency service agency.

_____   _____

Parent signature to acknowledge receipt   Date

_____   _____

Administrator signature   Date

BOLTING PROTOCOL

Bolting
Bolting is defined as:
_____
Example definition: any instance in which a student leaves the staff or building without permission after attempted de-escalation strategies and requests for student to remain in the designated area in the building.

When to follow the bolting protocol
1. When the student physically goes past the following boundaries:
2. _____
• *Example:* when he or she opens any school door and has at least one foot out of the door or when at recess, the student proceeds past the tree line of the playground.
3. When the student's behavior has escalated and he or she is moving toward the above-mentioned boundaries.

Important considerations
• [All staff assigned to an exit post and/or all staff working with a student with a history of bolting] will have a [walkie-talkie or cell phone] *on them at all times.*
• *Tip:* If cell phones are to be used for emergency situations, staff members should have updated phone numbers available at all times and should ensure that their phones work in all parts of school property.
• *Tip:* If walkie-talkies are to be used for emergency situations, staff members should ensure that the devises work in all parts of school property and check batteries daily.
• To initiate the bolting procedure, _____ will notify staff members to get to their posts via [loudspeaker announcement, walkie-talkie, cell phone].

Deciding whether to follow the student or physically stop the student from bolting

If the student is in *serious or imminent* danger, *physically stop the student.*

(Serious or imminent danger is defined as _____.)

Example: if the student is about to run into a busy street.

Otherwise, *follow the* student, and stay within sight of him or her.

Staff responsibilities and exits

- The crisis leader is: _____.
- Other crisis team members are:

    • _____
    • _____
    • _____

A designated staff member and substitute will be assigned to a "post" near each exit in the building, in the case of an incident of bolting.

   Tip: Each exit should be named in a way that it is easy for all staff to identify.

   Example: Exit 1 post, cafeteria door; exit 2 post, door next to custodian's office

Exit 1 _____
   Primary person: _____
   Substitute person: _____
Exit 2 _____
   Primary person: _____
   Substitute person: _____
Exit 3 _____
   Primary person: _____
   Substitute person: _____
Exit 4 _____
   Primary person: _____
   Substitute person: _____

Name and identify staff for every exit in the building.

Bolting procedure

1. The staff member who notices the student bolting will swiftly follow the student.

2. *At the same time*, he or she will announce that the student has bolted (with a cell phone or walkie-talkie) or ask the closest staff member to do so by: _____ [notifying the office to make an announcement, or making an announcement on the walkie-talkie].

3. The secretary or designee will communicate via [intercom, walkie-talkie] to staff that they need to get to their posts. The statement used to communicate this will be: _____.

4. Staff will continue to follow student, keeping him or her within sight, and will communicate the location of the student to staff via [walkie-talkie, cell phone].

5. A second staff member (who is closest but preferably a crisis team member) should attempt to triangulate the student. For example, if staff member A follows the student out the cafeteria door, staff member B should run out the front door and try to cut the student off and/or corral the student back toward A.

6. This strategy can be communicated with walkie-talkies or cell phones.

7. If a staff member finds the student more than thirty feet from the building, the staff member will wait there with the student until a second or third crisis team member arrives. The crisis team member will wait with the student until the child is calm enough to return to class. If the student is not calm, the crisis team will decide whether to follow the safety protocol.

8. The student's parents will be notified of the incident on the same day that the behavior incident occurs.

Parent/guardian notification

The student's parent or guardian will be called by the staff on the same day that the behavior incident occurs.

The crisis leader or designee will contact the parent or guardian. If a staff member doesn't reach the parent personally, staff will leave a voicemail and try to contact the parent or guardian again within the school day.

If student is missing for ten minutes or more
1. _____ will contact [school principal, headmaster] immediately. 2. _____ will contact parent or guardian within ___minutes of noticing student has been gone for ___ minutes (___ minutes after realizing student is missing). If staff member connects to parent's voicemail, leave message explaining student has left the premises or cannot be found and continue to try to reach the parent or guardian. 3. _____ will call local police department if the student has been missing for __ minutes.

Documentation
Any staff involved with or witness to the behavior incident will fill out incident forms (or restraint/seclusion forms if necessary) on the same day the incident occurred. Copies will be sent to parent or guardian and administration.

Emergency protocol

If student exhibits unsafe behavior in the following ways, the emergency protocol will be initiated:
 	
_____
 	
1. Staff will follow safety protocol.
 	
2. Staff will call student's parent or guardian *and* will call:
  • _____ [911 or mental health emergency service agency]
  • Parent phone number: _____
  • Mental health emergency service agency phone number:
  _____
 	
3. If staff doesn't reach the parent or guardian personally, staff will leave a message while another staff member calls 911 or mental health emergency service agency. If parent has previously agreed, contact the sequence of emergency contact numbers provided by the parent or guardian after calling 911 or mental health emergency service agency.

_____   _____
Parent signature to acknowledge receipt   Date

_____   _____
Administrator signature   Date

THREAT PROTOCOL

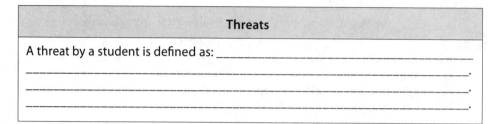

Threats
A threat by a student is defined as: _____ _____. _____. _____.

When to use threat protocol
Any time a student makes a verbal or nonverbal threat (as defined above) toward a student or staff member. *Act fast.* *Take it seriously.* *Report **any** threat.* *If student makes an immediate threat with a weapon,* *immediately call 911 and contact the crisis leader.*

Important considerations
1. Assume *all* threats and attempts are serious, and report them immediately. 2. After the threat, do *not* leave the student unattended at any time.   *Tip*: Staff may want to specify a bathroom procedure so that the student is never out of the sight of a staff member. 3. Create an environment that is safe and calm and where trained personnel should attempt to calm the student. 4. If the threat occurs at the end of the school day, a staff members *stays with the student* until the staff member connects with the parent or guardian and, with the parent or guardian, decides on a plan for how the student will leave school (e.g., the student will not take the bus home but will wait with school staff in the office until a parent arrives).

What to do if a threat is made

1. Report the threat to your supervisor *immediately*.
2. *Mental health staff* (school-based or from a neighboring school or agency) will administer a *threat assessment* and determine if threat is *low, medium,* or *high*.

   Note: This protocol is not a threat assessment. The threat assessment needs to be supplemented and completed only by a mental health professional.
3. Follow the corresponding *threat procedure* for the appropriate threat level: *low, medium,* or *high*.

The threat assessment

Tip: The people qualified to make a threat assessment may include social workers, school psychologists, or other mental health staff. If no mental health staff is available, specify who else could assess the threat, such as the principal or a psychologist from another school or an outside agency.

Once the mental health staff defines the threat as low, medium, or high, follow the corresponding procedure listed below.

Low-level threat

A low-level threat is defined as: _____.

Example definition: Risk to target(s), students, staff, and school safety is minimal

After a trained mental health professional has determined the student has made a low-level threat, follow this procedure:

1. Contact the *parent or guardian*. If you connect to voicemail, leave a message stating that the student has made a threat at school, and continue to try to reach the parent or guardian every ten minutes.

   Parent phone number: _____
2. Identify appropriate interventions, and document the intervention plan.

Medium-level threat

A medium-level threat is defined as: _____.

After a trained mental health professional has determined the student has made a medium-level threat, follow this procedure:

1. Contact the parent or guardian. If you connect to voicemail, leave a message stating that the student has made a serious threat at school, and continue to try to reach the parent or guardian every ten minutes.

   Parent phone number: _____

2. A trained mental health professional or designee will remain with the student for the remainder of the school day.

3. _____ [staff member who witnessed the threat] will notify _____ [administrator] and _____ [the crisis leader] within ___ minutes.

   Phone numbers: _____

4. If the trained mental health professional deems it necessary to call *emergency mental health services*, for emergency support and evaluation, or 911, the building administrator or trained mental health professional will make this phone call.

   Emergency mental health service agency phone number: _____

5. Identify appropriate interventions, and document the intervention plan.

High-level threat

A high-level threat is defined as: _____.

After a trained mental health professional has determined the student has made a high-level threat, follow this procedure:

> *If student makes an immediate threat with a weapon,*
> *immediately call 911 and contact the crisis leader.*

1. The trained mental health professional will contact _____ [crisis leader] and _____ [building administrator] immediately.

2. A trained mental health professional and/or an administrator and crisis team will remain with the student for the remainder of the school day.

3. Contact the parent or guardian. If you connect to voicemail, leave a message stating that the student has made a serious threat at school, and continue to try to reach the parent or guardian every ten minutes.

   Parent phone number: _____

4. If the trained mental health professional deems it necessary to call *emergency mental health services*, for emergency support and evaluation, or 911, the building administrator or trained mental health professional will make this phone call.

    Emergency mental health service agency phone number:

    _____

5. Identify appropriate interventions, and document intervention plan.

Documentation

Any staff involved with or witness to the behavior incident will fill out incident forms (or restraint/seclusion forms if necessary) on the same day the incident occurred. Copies will be sent to parent or guardian and administration.

Emergency protocol

If student exhibits unsafe behavior in the following ways, the emergency protocol will be initiated: _____ _____.

1. Staff will follow safety protocol.

2. Staff will call student's parent or guardian ***and*** will call:
   - _____ [911 or mental health emergency service agency]
   - Parent phone number: _____
   - Mental health emergency service agency phone number: _____

3. If staff doesn't reach the parent or guardian personally, staff will leave a message while another staff member calls 911 or mental health emergency service agency. If parent has previously agreed, contact the sequence of emergency contact numbers provided by the parent or guardian after calling 911 or mental health emergency service agency..

_____   _____

Parent signature to acknowledge receipt   Date

_____   _____

Administrator signature   Date

SELF-HARM PROTOCOL

Suicide or self-harm
A suicide or self-harm statement is defined as: _____ _____.
Attempted suicide/self-harm is defined as: _____ _____.

When to use the self-harm protocol
• *Any time* a family member, a peer, a staff member, another adult, or the student himself or herself reports that this student has *made suicidal statements, attempted suicide, or communicated the intent to commit suicide,* verbally or in writing. • *Any time* a family member, a peer, a staff member, another adult, or the student himself or herself reports that this student is engaging in or contemplating engaging in *self-injurious behaviors.* Signs of self-injurious behaviors may include visible scars, bruises, lacerations, or abrasions. • *Other:* _____. <div align="center">*Then act fast* *Take it seriously* *Report any risk*</div>

What to do if you are aware of a suicide risk
1. Report the threat to your *supervisor*. 2. *Mental health staff* (school-based or from a neighboring school or agency) will administer a *self-harm assessment* and determine if risk is *low, medium,* or *high*. 　　*Note:* This protocol is not a self-harm assessment. The self-harm assessment needs to be supplemented by a mental health professional only. 3. Follow the corresponding *suicide risk procedure* for the appropriate risk level.

Important considerations

1. Assume *all* suicide attempts or statements are serious, and report them immediately.
2. After a suicide-risk statement or action, do *not* leave the student unattended at any time.

   Tip: Staff may want to specify a bathroom procedure so that the student is never out the of the sight of a staff member.
3. Create an environment to ensure that the student feels *safe* and where trained personnel should attempt to calm the student.
4. If the suicide-risk statement or action occurs at the end of the school day, a staff member needs to *stay with the student* in school until a staff member connects with the parent or guardian and, with the parent or guardian, makes plans for the student to go elsewhere and which adult will escort them.

The suicide or self-harm assessment

Tip: The people qualified to assess the risk of suicide or self-harm may include social workers, school psychologists, or other mental health staff. If no mental health staff is available, specify who else could assess the risk of suicide or self-harm, such as the principal or a psychologist from another school or an outside agency.

Once the mental health staff determines that there is a suicide or self-harm risk, follow the corresponding procedure listed below.

Low-level risk

A low-level risk is defined as: _____.

After a trained mental health professional has determined the student is at a low risk level, follow this procedure:

1. _____ will notify _____ [administrator] and _____ [crisis leader] within ___ minutes.
2. Phone numbers of case manager and administrator: _____.
   Staff will closely supervise student for the rest of the school day.
3. Contact the parent or guardian. If you connect to voicemail, leave a message stating that the student has made a self-harm statement at school, and continue to try to reach the parent or guardian every ten minutes.

   Parent phone number: _____
4. Identify appropriate interventions, and document the intervention plan.

Medium- or high-level risk

A medium- or high-level risk is defined as: _____.

After a trained mental health professional has determined the student is at a medium or high risk level, follow this procedure:

1. The mental health professional will contact the crisis team and the building administrator immediately.

2. A trained mental health professional and/or the administrator and crisis team will remain with the student for the remainder of the school day. Staff may want to specify a bathroom procedure so that the student is never out of the sight of a staff member.

3. Contact the *parent or guardian*. If you connect to voicemail, leave a message saying that the student has made a self-harm statement or attempt at school, and continue to try to reach the parent or guardian every ten minutes.

   Parent phone number: _____

4. If the trained mental health professional deems it necessary to call *emergency mental health services* for emergency support and evaluation, the building administrator or trained mental health professional will make this phone call.

   Emergency mental health service agency phone number:
   _____

5. Identify appropriate interventions, and document the intervention plan.

Documentation

Any staff involved with or witness to the behavior incident will fill out incident forms (or restraint/seclusion forms if necessary) on the same day the incident occurred. Copies will be sent to parent or guardian and administration.

Emergency protocol

If student exhibits unsafe behavior in the following ways, the emergency protocol will be initiated:

1. Staff will follow safety protocol.

2. Staff will call student's parent or guardian **and** will call:

   _____ [911 or mental health emergency service agency]

   Parent phone number: _____

   Mental health emergency service agency phone number: _____

3. If staff doesn't reach the parent or guardian personally, staff will leave a message while another staff member calls 911 or mental health emergency service agency. If parent has previously agreed, contact the sequence of emergency contact numbers provided by the parent or guardian after calling 911 or mental health emergency service agency.

_____   _____
Parent signature to acknowledge receipt   Date

_____   _____
Administrator signature   Date

Helpful Apps

The apps listed here are available for iOS, Android devices, or both. More information can be found by googling the name of the app.

SELF-REGULATION

At Ease: Relieves anxiety and worry through meditation, mental exercises, and journaling. Goal is deep, lasting change.

Autism 5-Point Scale EP: Helps users with autism spectrum disorders and other disabilities to communicate and regulate in emergency situations.

Breathe, Think, Do: App developed by Sesame Street, helps students calm down and solve everyday problems by helping a monster take big breaths, think of a plan, and try it out.

Digital Problem Solver: Teaches users to identify emotions of characters and to help characters self-regulate.

MindShift: Mobile anxiety coach, includes strategies to deal with anxiety-producing situations.

PTSD Coach: Provides information about post-traumatic stress disorder (PTSD) and tools for screening, symptom tracking, and symptom management.

Self-Regulation Training Board: Teaches self-regulation skills in physical, emotional, and cognitive domains.

Sōsh, Sōsh Lite: Self-regulation tools including the Shredder ("shreds" negative thoughts or feelings) and Voice Meter (light that gives students visual feedback on the volume of their voice).

Squeeze and Shake Stress Relief: Virtual stress ball that either looks and squeaks like a rubber ducky when you squeeze the screen or vibrates for a hand massage when you shake the phone.

Stop Panic & Anxiety Self-Help: Tools to help people with panic disorder, including a diary and audio clips for emotion training audio for calming, relaxation, and panic-attack assistance.

Stress Tracker: Stress management app that tracks stress, moods, sources of stress, and behaviors. View trends and suggested action steps.

SuperBetter: Tool created by game designers to build personal resilience. Aims to build physical, mental, emotional, and social strength during difficult times or life changes.

Tactical Breather: Provides training and practice at gaining control of stress responses, including heart rate, emotions, and concentration.

The Feelings Book: Teaches emotional identification, understanding, and regulation. Has three developmental levels.

The Shredder: App with only the Shredder tool from Sōsh.

Unstuck: Helps user get "from stuck to unstuck," no matter what the problem is, by identifying what kind of stuck moment the user is having and suggesting how to proceed.

Worry Box: Anxiety Self-Help: Creates a "worry box" to "put worries away"; list steps to manage worry or to find coping statements to think about the worry differently.

Zones of Regulation: Helps students categorize their emotions and levels of alertness into "zones" and teaches skills for self-regulation.

SELF-MONITORING AND MOOD TRACKING

AWARENESS: Alerts students to rate their emotions and provides coping strategies if needed.

Depression CBT Self-Help Guide: Includes a diary to monitor mood, suggestions based on cognitive behavioral therapy for battling depression, and emotion-training and relaxation audio.

Goal Streaks: Tracks the days that a goal is attained, and allows user to track "streaks."

I am Feeling . . . : Notifies users to log how they are currently feeling and creates a shareable history.

Moody Me: Mood Diary and Tracker: Tracks moods over time and allows users to store photos of what makes them happy or sad.

MotivAider: Calls attention to a desired behavior on a set schedule, with vibration and/or audible tone.

My Daily Journal: Journaling app with support for photos, online backup, and PDF export.

Percentally: Data collection app that collects tally data and automatically converts it to percentages.

Repeat Timer: Repeating interval timer.

Streaks: Tracks "streaks" of progress toward behavior goals.

Sym Trend: Diary that records health information for depression, attention deficit hyperactivity disorder (ADHD), or autism to help users understand patterns and triggers, see how treatment is working, and manage their own care

T2 Mood Tracker: Tool to monitor and track emotions (on provided or custom scales) over time.

Tally Counter: Tracks behavior frequency using tallies.

TracknShare: Allows user to track information such as symptoms, goals, mood, or habits.

VIDEO MODELING

Functional Planning System: Uses video modeling to plan a user's day.

My Pictures Talk: Video modeling tool.

Video Scheduler: Allows user to construct picture and video schedules.

CREATING STORIES TO TEACH STRATEGIES AND SOCIAL SKILLS

Between the Lines: Allows user to practice interpreting vocal intonation, facial expressions, perspective-taking, body language, and idiomatic or slang expressions using photographs and voices.

Choiceworks: Helping children complete daily routines (morning, day, and night); understand and control their feelings; and improve their waiting skills (taking turns and not interrupting).

Feel Electric!: Game created by Sesame Street to explore emotions and build expressive vocabulary skills.

iCreate . . . Social Skills Stories: Allows user to customize sequential steps of a storyline for individuals that need help building their social skills.

Pictello: Develops visual stories and talking books based on a series of pictures (from library or user photos). Can be used for stories to teach social skills and strategies, schedules, and language learning.

Social Skill Builder: Promotes social learning in individuals with learning challenges, using real video scenarios and multiple-choice questions.

Stories About Me: Creates talking picture books using photos, text, and voice recordings.

Stories2Learn: Creates personalized stories using photos, text, and audio messages.

StoryMaker for Social Stories: App for creating and presenting social stories.

BIOFEEDBACK

Emwave: Biofeedback software with handheld device. Includes breathing exercises and emotion visualizer.

GPS for the Soul: Measures heart rate and heart rate variability, and provides media, including music, poetry, and photos, and breathing exercises to help reduce stress.

iBiofeedback: Provides healing modules from different traditions, including chanting, meditation, and sound healing.

Stress Check: Uses device's camera to estimate user's stress level.

Stresseraser: Handheld biofeedback device.

BEHAVIOR AND DATA COLLECTION

123TokenMe: Personalizable reinforcement tool and data collection.

ABC Data Pro: Data collection tool for behavior and/or event counting, partial interval recording, full interval recording, and ABC (antecedent, behavior, and consequence) recording.

Autism: ABC Checklist Mobile App: Enables the recording of antecedent, behavior, duration, setting, and consequence. In addition, enables educator to produce an easy-to-follow log of information to aid in the analysis of any patterns to determine an intervention (if needed). Can easily be customized to meet teacher's requirements.

Autism: Duration Data Sheet Mobile App: Data sheet app created for specific students. Can be adapted or modified to fit student's needs, and can also be used as a template for teacher's own data sheets.

Behavior Support App: Behavior support for autism and special education. Helps user label target behaviors, identify function of behaviors, and begin to develop positive behavior support plans.

Behavior Tracker Pro: Allows user to track behavior and generate graphs and charts. Mobile app links to online portal for team use.

Catalyst Client: Behavior data collection app that syncs to web-based portal for storage and analysis.

Class Dojo: Allows teacher to give students positive behavior feedback points on strategy use or skill practice. Parents can also check in on student progress. Provides analytics and reports.

Ecove: Allows user to gather classroom observation data, including timers, counters, and checklists. Several apps available for different purposes.

iearnedthat: Behavior chart app that turns a picture of a reward into an interactive jigsaw of up to sixty pieces. User earns the reward one piece at a time for using strategies and skill practice.

Intervals: An ABA Interval Recording App: Performs ABA interval recordings and time samplings.

No More Meltdowns: Diary to record information relating to meltdowns and to analyze to see patterns. Teaches adults to manage their own feelings to calmly help the child, strategies to deescalate and soothe the child in the moment, understand common triggers, and create plans to prevent future problems.

Teach Me Skills Advanced: Collects data on skill acquisition and behavior intervention.

EXECUTIVE FUNCTIONING

7Notes HD Premium: Note-taking app with handwriting recognition.

Colornote: Simple note-taking app. Includes checklist creation, notes in calendar, and syncing.

Evernote: Enables user to create notes with text, photos, lists, or voice reminders. Notes can be shared, searched, and organized.

Fotobabble: Creates "talking photos" with user's photos and recorded messages. Can be used to make a future picture for students or to create a positive self-talk picture or to remind a student of a strategy.

Goodnotes: Allows user to take notes and annotate PDF documents.

My Video Schedule: Users can create video schedule using large provided library of photos and videos or creating their own.

Notability: Note-taking app that also allows editing of PDFs and Google Docs. Notes can be linked to audio recordings.

Picture Scheduler: Task organizer with option of text, picture, audio, or video tasks. Includes alarm function and recurring alarms.

Tellagami: Creates simple animated videos. Can be used to make a future picture for students.

Timer+: Set multiple timers at once. Program minute, hour, or second.

Traffic Light: Timer goes from green to yellow to red as user runs out of time.

VisTimer: Gentle implementation of time-imposed limits. Utilizes an animated shrinking pie chart to depict elapsed time. Visual thinkers, especially children, have difficulty conceptualizing time.

VoCal: Creates audio to-do list with no need for writing.

PREVIEWING

Edmodo: Social platform for education; allows secure discussions, posting of assignments, and file sharing. Students can use app to preview the class when they are outside the classroom and to participate in class without having to speak in front of peers.

Facetime: Video calling app.

iPrompts: An app to rapidly create and present visual cues that help individuals make the transition from one activity to the next, understand upcoming events, make choices, focus on the task at hand, and learn social skills.

Skype: Cross-platform video and voice calling app.

Socrative Teacher: Class engagement tool providing games and exercises. Students can use it to participate from outside the classroom and to participate in class without having to speak in front of peers.

DEPRESSION AND OTHER NEGATIVE THINKING

Anti-Stress Quotes: Displays quotes about success, motivation, perseverance, courage, inspiration, and hope. Allows users to save and share favorites.

Depression CBT Self-Help Guide: Includes a diary to monitor mood, suggestions based on cognitive behavioral therapy for battling depression, and emotion-training and relaxation audio.

Depression Inventory: Weekly test to track depressive moods over time.

depressioncheck: Three-minute checklist that screens for depression.

Operation Reach Out: A lifesaving app for iPhone and Android; developed by the military to prevent suicide. Encourages users who are having suicidal thoughts to reach out to others, and provides activities to help them stay connected. Recorded videos and menu options help users assess their thinking and reach out for help in crisis.

Positive Thinking: Provides positive phrases and reminders. Also allows users to add their own positive statements.

WRITING

Clicker 6: Word processor for students learning to read and write. Sentences created from pictures or words are read back to the student.

Dragon Dictation: Voice-recognition app that allows users to instantly see in writing what they have spoken.

Flying Books: Children's books read by a narrator or recorded by user. Can create book using photos or artwork.

Kidblog: Allows students to have protected blogs where they can post and participate in discussions. Teachers have complete control over student blogs.

Kidspiration Maps: Allows students to create visual maps to build reading, writing, and thinking skills. Transforms pictures into written words.

Popplet: Creates visual mind-maps that capture thoughts and images and create relationships between them. Can be used for collaborative brainstorming, and students can leave comments on one another's work.

Read & Write: Web app for Google Chrome that adds accessibility options to Google Docs, PDFs, e-books, and the web. Includes read-aloud function, highlighter, picture dictionary, talking dictionary, and vocabulary builder.

Ready to Print: Teaches handwriting skills to pre-writers.

Story Builder: Allows user to record audio narrative based on story prompts.

Typ-O: Uses word prediction and spelling error prevention to help prevent typos and make writing easier.

CALMING

Acupressure: Heal Yourself: Illustrated instructions for acupressure point massage.

breeze: realistic wind chimes: Interactive wind chimes with relaxing background sounds.

Calm Myself Down: Uses ABA (applied behavior analysis) techniques to help user (particularly those with autism spectrum disorders) stay calm and in control.

Calming Music to Simplicity: Plays Chinese traditional music for calming and relaxation.

Dropophone: Allows user to combine sounds of rain falling on different tiny instruments by tapping pictures of raindrops.

Fluid: Turns device screen into an interactive pool of water.

Laser Lights : Laser light effects controlled by user.

MeMoves: App intended to complement DVD. User completes "finger puzzles" to the beat of calming music. DVD has interactive "body puzzles" that combine music, movement, and images and can be used in school as a transition tool or priming activity for the whole class.

Monster Chorus: Cute monsters each sing a note; user can combine them to create songs.

Nature Sounds Relax and Sleep: Plays relaxing nature sounds.

Naturespace: "3-D" audio of nature sounds.

Ooze: User interacts with color-shifting "goo" by touching the screen and tilting the device.

PaintSparkle: Coloring book app with coloring pages and ability to color user's photos.

Pocket Pond 2: Soothing interactive koi pond with relaxing nature sounds.

Relax Melodies: Customizable white-noise app that mixes different sounds. Includes sleep timer.

Relax Ocean Waves Sleep: Ocean sounds for relaxation.

Relax with Andrew Johnson Lite: Provides relaxation audio.

Relaxing Sounds of Nature Lite: Nature sound app, includes ability to mix sounds.

Silk: Calming music plays while user creates soothing designs.

BREATHING

BellyBio Interactive Breathing: Biofeedback app that generates music in sync with deep belly breathing.

Breathe2Relax: Diaphragmatic breathing exercise for stress management.

Health Through Breath: Multilevel deep-breathing course for stress reduction.

Relax Lite: Stress Relief: Five-minute stress relief app that teaches deep breathing.

Universal Breathing: Pranayama: Guides user to breathe slowly and deeply.

MEDITATION

Buddhify: Teaches mindfulness meditation with guided meditations, including some for specific situations, including waking up, being in a park, working online, or going to sleep.

Cleveland Clinic Stress Free Now: Provides seven relaxation techniques, including breathing and meditation exercises.

Qi Gong Meditation Relaxation: Plays short videos teaching gentle Qi Gong movements and breathing exercises.

Relax and Rest Meditations: User can listen to meditation sessions of various lengths, with or without nature sounds or music.

Simply Being: Provides five- to twenty-minute meditation sessions with or without nature sounds or music.

Smiling Mind: Meditation app aimed at young people.

Take a Break! Guided Meditations for Stress Relief: Guided meditation audio.

FAIR Behavior Intervention Plan Template

Student's Name: _____   Date: _____

TARGETED BEHAVIORS (use measurable definitions only):

WARNING SIGNS (list behavior clues that indicate the student's behavior may be escalating):

F   **Functional Hypothesis**

Document all instances of targeted behaviors, using ABC data sheet (minimum of ten incidents):

Antecedents	*Consequences*
Setting Events of Note	

What is the functional hypothesis, according to ABC notes (can check more than one)?

☐ Escape   ☐ Sensory

☐ Tangible

☐ Attention

Accommodations

Environmental

Executive functioning

Curriculum	Replacement behaviors
Underdeveloped skill development	**Self-regulation and self-monitoring**

I **Interaction Strategies**

R **Response Strategies**

Bonus points assigned for the following strategies/skill practice:

1. _____
2. _____
3. _____
4. _____

DATA COLLECTION

List the target behaviors on which you will collect, or will continue to collect, data, and list which data sheets you will be using:

Also list timeline and review dates, including benchmarks and timelines for reviewing the FAIR Behavior Intervention Plan.

IMPLEMENTATION CHECKLIST

On a separate worksheet, create a corresponding implementation checklist.

FAIR PLAN COLLABORATION

Please list all involved team members and their roles in implementing the plan:

Staff _____   Role/responsibility: _____

Staff _____   Role/responsibility: _____

Staff _____   Role/responsibility: _____

SIGNATURES

_____   _____

Staff signature   Date

_____   _____

Parent/guardian signature   Date

Updated FAIR Behavior Intervention Plan for Students with Anxiety-Related Behavior

Student's Name: _____   Date: _____

TARGETED BEHAVIORS (be as explicit as possible):

WARNING SIGNS (list behavior clues that indicate the student's behavior may be escalating):

F Functional Hypothesis

Document all instances of targeted behaviors, using ABC data sheet (minimum of ten incidents):

Antecedents	Consequences
Setting Events of Note	

What is the functional hypothesis, according to ABC notes (can check more than one)?

☐ Escape   ☐ Attention

☐ Tangible   ☐ Sensory

A Accommodations

Environmental

- ☐ Provide safe space in classroom
- ☐ Schedule regular breaks
- ☐ Allow for breaks outside the classroom
- ☐ Arrange alternative lunch
- ☐ Arrange alternative recess
- ☐ Provide other areas of competence (specify):

  _____
- ☐ Other:

Executive functioning

- ☐ Teach "reading the room"
- ☐ Use visual timer
- ☐ Narrate passage of time
- ☐ Use segmented clock
- ☐ Consider untimed test
- ☐ Use visual schedules
- ☐ Put organization time in schedule
- ☐ Present only a few problems or items at a time
- ☐ Preview nonpreferred tasks in the morning
- ☐ Consider accommodated or modified homework
- ☐ Use of technology:

  _____
- ☐ Other:

Curriculum

- ☐ Use pictures to help student think of and maintain a topic when they write
- ☐ Have student use word processing
- ☐ Consider spelling accommodations
- ☐ Other curriculum support: _____
- ☐ Other technology support: _____

Writing

☐ Have student use self-monitoring writing strategies checklist

☐ Use the rating system for writing (or other anxiety-provoking academic subject)

☐ Use "How I Feel About Writing" sheet (see chapter 4)

☐ Use of technology:

_____

Replacement behaviors (examples for attention-motivated behavior):

☐ Teach asking for a break appropriately

☐ Teach asking for help appropriately

☐ Use of technology:

_____

☐ Other:

Teaching underdeveloped skills

☐ Positive thinking

☐ Executive functioning

☐ Self-regulation

☐ Social skills

☐ Use of technology:

_____

☐ Other:

Self-regulation and self-monitoring

☐ Have student use regulation scale (i.e., emotional thermometer)

☐ Prompt for "body check" cues throughout the day

☐ Have student develop and use calming box

☐ Have student use self-regulation chart: "what to do when I feel . . ."

☐ Have student use mobile device for self-monitoring

☐ Use the self-monitoring sheet

☐ Other self-monitoring strategies: _____

Self-calming instruction and practice

☐ Have the student practice self-calming (specify how many times per day or week, and for how long)

☐ Use visual self-regulation list

☐ Use self-evaluation data sheet

☐ Use of technology: _____

Breaks

☐ Create data sheet to determine helpful break choices and if breaks are working throughout day, or visual list to help the student make helpful break choices

☐ Use cognitive distraction break choices (decision based on data)

☐ Schedule breaks—noncontingent escape to prevent avoidance behavior (specify before, after, and during activity and how many per day)

☐ Create break cards or strategy cards for student to use

☐ Use of technology: _____

☐ Other:

I Interaction Strategies

General interaction

☐ Use concise language

☐ Apply noncontingent reinforcement

☐ Use leadership-building and self-esteem-building activities

☐ Work on explicit relationship building

☐ Use validation

☐ Use of technology:

_____

☐ Other:

Catching Them Early

☐ Respond to any sudden change in behavior with supportive response

☐ Use verbal check-in

☐ Use Thought Journals

☐ Use daily check-in sheet

☐ Use of technology:

_____

☐ Other:

Transitions

☐ Develop transition plan

☐ Support abrupt transitions; use graduated transition strategies:

_____

☐ Include transition warnings: _____

☐ Include transition accommodations: _____

☐ To support stopping: _____

☐ To support cognitive shifting: _____

☐ To support starting/initiating: _____

☐ To support downtime/wait-time: _____

☐ Include explicit instruction for transitions: _____

☐ Use of technology: _____

☐ Other:

R Response Strategies

For escape-motivated behavior

☐ Avoid responses that would reinforce escape-motivated behavior, such as time-outs and removal from class

☐ Avoid requiring student to earn escape or breaks; provide breaks noncontingently

☐ Prompt student to use a strategy when student shows signs of anxiety

☐ Assign rewards or points when the student demonstrates a strategy, a self-regulation skill, or a replacement behavior

☐ Avoid rewards or consequences based on consistent or set behavior criteria (behavior performance)

☐ Label the student's anxiety level when the student shows signs of anxiety

☐ Remind the student of previous success at calming

☐ Exposure: if a student exhibits low tolerance for work, start in small increments and allow escape from work (break), and build up workload slowly

☐ Use of technology: _____

☐ Other:

Bonus points assigned for the following strategies/skill practice:

1. _____

2. _____

3. _____

4. _____

DATA COLLECTION

List the target behaviors on which you will collect, or will continue to collect, data, and list which data sheets you will be using:

Also list timeline and review dates, including benchmarks and timelines for reviewing the FAIR Behavior Intervention Plan.

IMPLEMENTATION CHECKLIST

On a separate worksheet, create a corresponding implementation checklist.

FAIR BEHAVIOR INTERVENTION PLAN COLLABORATION

Please list all involved team members and their roles in implementing the plan:

Staff _____ Role/responsibility: _____

Staff _____ Role/responsibility: _____

Staff _____ Role/responsibility: _____

SIGNATURES

_____   _____
Staff signature   Date

_____   _____
Parent/guardian signature   Date

Updated FAIR Behavior Intervention Plan for Students with Oppositional Behavior

Student's Name: _____   Date: _____

TARGETED BEHAVIORS (be as explicit as possible):

WARNING SIGNS (list behavior clues that indicate the student's behavior may be escalating):

F Functional Hypothesis

Document all instances of targeted behaviors, using ABC data sheet (minimum of ten incidents):

Antecedents	*Consequences*
Setting Events of Note	

What is the functional hypothesis, according to ABC notes (can check more than one)?

- ☐ Escape
- ☐ Tangible
- ☐ Attention
- ☐ Sensory

A Accommodations

Strategies and interventions from other chapters that you may consider are included.

Environmental

- ☐ Provide safe space in classroom
- ☐ Modify schedule
- ☐ Schedule breaks
- ☐ Allow for breaks outside the classroom
- ☐ Arrange alternative recess
- ☐ Arrange alternative lunch
- ☐ Provide other areas of competence:

  –––––––––––––––––––––––

- ☐ Other:

Executive functioning

- ☐ Teach "reading the room"
- ☐ Use visual timer
- ☐ Narrate passage of time
- ☐ Use segmented clock
- ☐ Consider untimed test
- ☐ Use visual schedules
- ☐ Put organization time in schedule
- ☐ Present only a few problems or items at a time
- ☐ Use of technology:

  –––––––––––––––––––––––

- ☐ Other:

Curriculum

- ☐ Embed choice
- ☐ Alternate easy and difficult assignments
- ☐ Have student use word processing
- ☐ Consider spelling accommodations
- ☐ Assess quality, not quantity, of work
- ☐ Offer hands-on, experiential lessons
- ☐ Give open-ended, flexible assignments
- ☐ Use student's own interests in curriculum
- ☐ Use of technology:

  –––––––––––––––––––––––

- ☐ Other:

Writing

- ☐ Have student use self-monitoring writing strategies checklist
- ☐ Use the rating system for writing (or other anxiety-provoking academic subject)
- ☐ Use "How I Feel About Writing" sheet (see chapter 4)
- ☐ Use of technology:

  _____
- ☐ Other:

Teaching underdeveloped skills

- ☐ Positive thinking
- ☐ Self-monitoring
- ☐ Flexible thinking
- ☐ Executive functioning
- ☐ Self-regulation
- ☐ Social skills
- ☐ Use of technology:

  _____
- ☐ Other:

Self-regulation and self-monitoring

- ☐ Have student use emotional thermometer
- ☐ Prompt for "body checks" throughout the day
- ☐ Have student develop and use calming box
- ☐ Have student use self-regulation chart
- ☐ Use the self-monitoring sheet
- ☐ Other:

Replacement behaviors (examples for attention-motivated behavior):

- ☐ Teach asking for a break appropriately
- ☐ Teach asking for help appropriately
- ☐ Other:

Self-calming instruction and practice

☐ Have the student practice self-calming (specify how many times per day or week, and for how long)

☐ Use visual self-regulation list

☐ Use self-evaluation data sheet

☐ Use of technology:

_____

☐ Other:

Breaks

☐ Create data sheet to determine helpful break choices and if breaks are working throughout the day

☐ Create a break menu or visual list to help the student make helpful break choices

☐ Use cognitive distraction break choices (decision based on data)

☐ Schedule breaks—noncontingent escape from demands to minimize frustration (specify before, after, and during activity and how many per day)

☐ Create break cards or strategy cards for student to use

☐ Use of technology:

_____

☐ Other:

❙ Interaction Strategies

General interaction

☐ Use strength-based terminology

☐ Work on explicit relationship building

☐ Use intermittent reinforcement

☐ Use noncontingent reinforcement

☐ Use leadership-building and self-esteem-building activities

☐ Use validation

☐ Prompt student to avoid asking yes-or-no questions and to ask in a different way

☐ Other:

Transitions:

☐ Develop transition plan

☐ Support abrupt transitions; use graduated transition strategies:

_____

☐ Include transition warnings: _____

☐ Include transition accommodations: _____

☐ To support stopping: _____

☐ To support cognitive shifting: _____

☐ To support starting/initiating: _____

☐ To support downtime or wait time: _____

☐ Include explicit instruction for transitions: _____

☐ Use of technology: _____

☐ Other:

Strategies for giving demands

☐ Avoid power struggles

☐ Avoid yes-or-no questions or saying, "OK?" when making a demand

☐ Embed choice in the demand

☐ Use declarative language

☐ Give indirect demands

☐ Give demand, and move away

☐ Give extended time for compliance

☐ Use humor when appropriate

☐ Make it a game

☐ Give direction privately

☐ Give direction nonverbally

☐ Preview the demand

☐ Provide the rationale first

☐ Switch adults

☐ Other:

To reduce negative-attention seeking from a teacher:

☐ Make positive reinforcement/ attention predictable

☐ Make positive reinforcement/ attention more efficient

☐ Make positive reinforcement/ attention more obvious

☐ Positively reinforce expected behavior

☐ Make positive reinforcement/ attention more dramatic/intense

☐ Have student agree to a positive attention system he or she is comfortable with

☐ Other:

R Response Strategies

☐ Assign rewards or points when the student demonstrates a self-regulation or prosocial skill when student is anxious or frustrated

☐ Answer simple questions

☐ Avoid ignoring the behavior

☐ Redirect challenging questions, and provide a limit

☐ Set limits that are enforceable, reasonable, and clear and simple

☐ Use incremental reinforcement systems

☐ Frustration tolerance: if a student exhibits low tolerance for work, start in building small increments, give escape from work (a break), and build up workload slowly

☐ Use processing sheet (specify when, in what format, and supported by whom) to teach, not to punish

☐ Use of technology: _____

☐ Other:

For escape-motivated behavior

☐ Avoid responses that would reinforce escape-motivated behavior, such as time-outs and removal from class

For attention-motivated behavior

☐ Avoid responses such as one-on-one talks or repeatedly telling the student to stop

For tangibly motivated behavior

☐ Avoid responses such as giving an object or allowing the student to do something after the child demands it inappropriately

Bonus points assigned for the following strategies/skill practice:

1. _____
2. _____
3. _____
4. _____

DATA COLLECTION

List the target behaviors on which you will collect, or will continue to collect, data, and list which data sheets you will be using:

Also list timeline and review dates, including benchmarks and timelines for reviewing the FAIR Behavior Intervention Plan.

IMPLEMENTATION CHECKLIST

On a separate worksheet, create a corresponding implementation checklist.

FAIR BEHAVIOR INTERVENTION PLAN COLLABORATION

Please list all involved team members and their roles in implementing the plan:

Staff _____   Role/responsibility: _____

Staff _____   Role/responsibility: _____

Staff _____   Role/responsibility: _____

SIGNATURES

_____   _____
Staff signature   Date

_____   _____
Parent/guardian signature   Date

APPENDIX G

Answer Key

There are no definitive answers to the situations and scenarios that arise when you are working with students with anxiety-related and oppositional behaviors. This section will provide you with some possible answers to consider for some of the reflection, practice, and case study exercises in this guide. If your answers don't match up, it doesn't mean they are wrong. There are no right answers; you must apply only what works for your student. I have provided these answers as an opportunity to reflect on some other possibilities.

CHAPTER 1

Practice: Reframing Our Understanding of Behavior

Misbehavior is a symptom of an underlying cause.

Possible ways to understand Joe's behavior include:

- Joe's social skills, specifically his ability to take turns, are underdeveloped. He needs practice and instruction in that area.
- Joe has difficulty waiting for his turn. Waiting is an underdeveloped skill and needs to be taught and accommodated.
- Joe misperceived the social situation, and when he observed students pushing one another on the swing, he thought pushing was OK. He needs to be taught the rules of pushing kids on the swing.
- Joe's social skills are underdeveloped in the area of initiating an interaction. Joe might have pushed Keiko to initiate a social interaction. He needs instruction on how to initiate conversation or other interaction.

Behavior is communication.

Possible ways to understand Joe's behavior include:

- Joe may be communicating through behavior that he wants a turn on the swing. He needs to be taught another way to communicate this (i.e., functional communication).
- Joe may have wanted to communicate a greeting or social initiation when he pushed Keiko off the swing.
- Joe may be communicating that it's hard for him to wait (he's frustrated) until students are done with the swing and he is confused as to how long each student gets on the swing.
- Joe might be communicating that taking turns is confusing and he needs more support during those instances.
- Joe might be communicating that unstructured times are stressful for him and he could use support.

Behavior has a function.

Possible ways to understand Joe's behavior include:

- Joe is successfully *escaping* having to wait for the swing.
- Joe is successfully *escaping* having to take turns or having to remember the social rules that go along with understanding that.
- Joe successfully attained negative *attention* from the peer and the teacher.

Behavior occurs in patterns.

ABC notes might show, among other things, that the following situations represent patterns and are often difficult for Joe:

- Having to take turns
- Having to wait
- Behavior incidents during social situations
- Behavior incidents during unstructured times

The only behavior that teachers can control is their own.

Possible ways to understand Joe's behavior include:

- The teacher can realize that yelling or complaining about the student near peers is not a productive response, and she can remind herself to use the situation as a teachable moment.

- The teacher can realize that she can control her response and give Joe private feedback so that other peers don't decide he's a bad kid.

Behavior can be changed.

Through social skills instruction, Joe can learn to take turns.

- By being taught to wait and with waiting accommodations, Joe can learn to successfully wait without incident.
- Through social skills instruction, Joe can learn to initiate with peers appropriately.
- Through practice, Joe can learn how to push students on the swing appropriately.

CHAPTER 2

Practice: Analyzing Juanita's ABC Notes

1. **What patterns do you notice in the antecedent column?**

   Demand (sweatshirt) /

   Social demand (math group, hallway) //

   Told no (bathroom at lunch) /

   English class //

   Transition (walking into English, dismissal in the hallway) //

   Unstructured (lunch, dismissal in the hallway) //

2. **What patterns, if any, do you notice with the setting events?**

   Frequent conflict in the home, including contact with biological mother, arguments with stepmother, and domestic disturbance.

3. **What patterns do you notice with time of day or activity?**

   No behavior incidents have occurred in the mornings (before 11:15 a.m.).

   English was an antecedent/activity twice.

   Half of the incidents occurred at 2:00pm or after.

4. **What patterns do you notice in the consequence column?**

   Removed from the room (went to office after sweatshirt incident, counselor instead of math group, principal's office instead of cafeteria) ///

Escaped demand (didn't take off hood, went to bathroom, didn't work with the group, slept through English—didn't do work) ////

Peers laughed (mimicked teacher, insulted peer in hallway) //

5. **What is your hypothesis of the function or functions of Juanita's behavior in light of these patterns?**

The function of Juanita's behavior is scape, negative attention, and something tangible. She is successfully escaping demands and activities (escape) Twice, she received negative attention from peers (negative attention), and four times, she didn't comply with demands, which allowed her to maintain her agenda (tangible).

Using ABC Information to Inform Practice

Let's say you are Juanita's teacher. Use the ABC notes to inform your practice.

1. **Are there any patterns with time of day or activities? If so, what interventions would you implement to address the patterns?**

Because behavior incidents are occurring after 11:15 a.m., Juanita might need scheduled breaks throughout the later morning and the afternoon. Alternative lunch should be considered for several reasons: her behavior escalated in the cafeteria, she has a pattern of undesirable behavior in the afternoon, and social demands are an antecedent. Two behavior incidents occurred in English class, so interventions should be brainstormed to help her during that class.

2. **Looking at the antecedent patterns in the ABC notes for Juanita, how would you change your interventions to prevent the student from engaging in unwanted behavior in the future?**

The teacher could provide accommodations and support during English class, support with social demands and small-group work. Juanita could also use support during transitions and unstructured times of the school day.

3. **What do you notice about the setting events? Do you need to check in with Juanita? Do you need to report any information to the principal or social worker or student's private therapist? Are you focusing on what you can do within the school day?**

Morning check-in would be helpful to assess what outside factors are contributing to her behavior. The teacher should tell the social worker and maybe the principal about the conflicts with Juanita's stepmother and about the biological mother's recent contact with Juanita. The principal and the social worker need to be told about the domestic disturbance at home. The teacher needs to have a consistent way of documenting all information from home.

4. **Looking at the consequence patterns in the ABC notes, how would you change your responses in the future so that you do not reinforce the function of Juanita's behavior?**

   Juanita is successfully escaping nonpreferred activities through inappropriate behavior. Teaching her a replacement behavior, an appropriate way to escape (e.g., teaching her to ask for a break or for help), will reduce inappropriate behavior. Interventions should be focused on weak subject matter, initiating difficult tasks, transitions, unstructured time, and navigating small-group work. The teacher should prompt these strategies before sending the student out of the room or should preview these strategies before an incident occurs.

Practice: Analyzing Raul's ABC Notes

1. **What patterns do you notice in the antecedent column?**

   Large group (chorus, recess) //

   Performance situation (chorus, putting paper on display) //

   Transitions (language arts twice, homework/dismissal) ///

   Language arts //

2. **What patterns, if any, do you notice with setting events?**

   Raul gets worked up about school and schoolwork at home. Raul had two behavior incidents on the days his babysitter was picking him up from school.

3. **What patterns do you notice with time of day or activity?**

   All incidents occurred in the late afternoon (after 1:15 p.m.). Two incidents occurred during language arts.

4. **What patterns do you notice in the consequence column?**

One-on-one attention from the teacher when Raul was spoken to (chorus, math, language arts twice, homework, extra recess) *### //*

Avoided demand or activity (chorus, math, language arts twice, homework, extra recess) *### //*

5. **What is your hypothesis of the function or functions of Raul's behavior in light of these patterns?**

He successfully avoided nonpreferred demand or activity in all instances (escape). He gained his teacher's attention in all instances (at least maintained by attention).

Using ABC Information to Inform Practice

Let's say you are Raul's teacher. Use the ABC notes to inform your practice.

1. **Are there any patterns with time of day or activities? If so, what interventions would you implement to address the patterns?**

Raul is struggling in the afternoons. Scheduled breaks, starting midday at least, will help him be more regulated in the afternoon. Language arts and transitions as well as performances are difficult for him.

2. **Looking at the antecedent patterns in the ABC notes for Raul, how would you change your interventions to prevent the student from engaging in unwanted behavior in the future?**

Language arts, large-group activities, transitions, and performance situations are antecedents/difficult situations. Interventions should focus on these areas and could include recess buddies and transition warnings or accommodations.

3. **What do you notice about the setting events? Do you need to check in with Raul? Do you need to report any information to the principal or social worker or the student's private therapist? Are you focusing on what you can do within the school day?**

Raul expresses stress about school and schoolwork at home. A morning check-in would be a great way to see if he is worried about something in particular that school day. Breaks throughout the day and support around antecedents will hopefully help his anxiety toward school. Raul had two behavior incidents when his babysitter was picking him up. Previewing this pickup arrangement with Raul during the day and letting the social worker know that this situation could be causing stress will be helpful, as would talking to his parent.

4. **Looking at the consequence patterns in the ABC notes, how would you change your responses in the future so that you do not reinforce the function of Raul's behavior?**

When Raul is not participating in the activity, instead of repeating the direction or reminding him of the expectation multiple times, the teacher could support his initiation of work or support him in the activity. Currently Raul is escaping demands and activities through inappropriate, less communicative behavior. Teaching Raul replacement behaviors such as asking for a break or for help would reduce the inappropriate behaviors.

Raul should not be required to perform publicly, or should be required to do so only rarely, until he is more comfortable with it. For example, he could be allowed to sit during chorus class without singing or he could show a friend his work instead of hanging it on the wall.

CHAPTER 3

Practice: Brainstorming Breaks

Concerns	Possible solutions or responses
1. If he takes a break, he'll be missing instruction.	• Have a buddy fill him in verbally when he returns.
	• Have a buddy take notes and hand them to the student when he returns.
	• Videotape the teacher so he can watch it when he returns.
	• Preview the lesson with student so he has heard it before and can jump in more easily if he misses a section.
	• Have his break take place in the classroom so he can listen while on break.
	• If he is very resistant to being in class and needs breaks outside the room, have him use a video chat app (e.g., FaceTime) to listen to instruction from a "safer" location. (Often, students who do this are able to rejoin the class once they hear what the class content will be.)

Concerns	Possible solutions or responses
	• Have the whole class take a break if the data shows it's helpful for the student.
	• Have a class member "review" for the class the instructions thus far when the student returns.
2. What if she refuses to come back to class from the break and gets upset?	• Avoid offering highly preferred activities during the break if these are hard to shift away from.
	• If you can schedule the break, have the student take a break right before a preferred activity (e.g., computer and then recess).
	• (See the "Transitions: Expanded" section in chapter 3 for more details on stopping and making transitions.
3. If I give him break cards so he can initiate breaks, he'll overuse them.	• Give him a maximum amount of break cards so he can budget.
	• Give him different hierarchical break cards (e.g. a quick-drink-of-water break, a ten-minute break, an opt-out-of-class break) so he can self-monitor the type of break he needs.
4. Who is going to supervise the breaks? I don't have a classroom assistant.	• Breaks can take place in the classroom as long as the data suggests they work.
	• Use the whole "village." Ask the principal if someone in the building could take the student for a break during math class. Often there is a solution.
	• The secretary and nurse offices typically have someone in attendance. Sending a student to visit them or deliver something to them will allow you to know there is an adult receiving them. Some teachers will text the nurse: "He's coming" and have her text back: "He's here."
	• Use a buddy class or buddy teacher (i.e., a nearby teacher who will allow the student to take a break in his or her classroom).
	• Have the student go for a walk with a peer if the data suggests that this would be helpful.

Concerns	Possible solutions or responses
5. But she didn't earn it . . .	• Breaks should not be earned, but should be noncontingent and thought of as an accommodation. • Using the metaphor of a person with a physical disability can highlight this point: we don't have to earn the right to wear glasses in class or take a bathroom break; it is understood that these accommodations are needed.
6. He exhibited inappropriate behavior right before break time so we didn't give it to him. We didn't want to reinforce the inappropriate behavior.	• This is a sign he may have needed a break earlier. • Even though the student is acting inappropriately, point out a minor compliance: "Oh, you stood up when I mentioned it was time for a break —thank you for listening." Then take him for a break. • Hold the conversation about the behavior incident until after the break.
7. Is it OK to have the child do something rewarding on a break?	• Yes, as long as the data suggests it is calming and regulating. • However, if the student has a very difficult time making the transition back to an activity, the activity may be too potent for the student, especially if it's a restricted interest of the student's.
8. I know she needs a break, and the breaks help her, but she refuses to go.	• Talk to the student, and have her suggest what she wants to do on a break and what is helpful. • Ask the student what she doesn't like about the break (e.g., social stigma, missing academics). • Sometimes the student associates the word *break* with something negative, and she reacts negatively: "I don't need a break!" Changing the word might promote compliance (e.g., "Why don't you take a minute"). • Transition objects can refocus the student from class to a break (see chapter 3 for details). • You can disguise the break as a task (e.g., "Can you bring this book to Ms. Jones?") as long as it's regulating.
9. Other?	

CHAPTER 4

Case Study: Analyzing Harry's Behavior Plan

1. **Are the target behaviors measurable? Do they represent behaviors that are appropriate and should be increased?**

   The target behaviors are measurable although they are not complete with examples and nonexamples. The target behaviors are inappropriate and are targeted to decrease.

2. **Is there a list of antecedents (collected from data) and corresponding interventions to reduce the student's anxiety in those activities or moments?**

   No.

3. **Is the functional hypothesis based on ABC notes or a functional behavior analysis, and is the hypothesis written on the plan?**

   No.

4. **What percentage of the plan is preventative, and what percentage is reactive?**

   There are only two preventative strategies, including previewing a visual schedule and specifying the amount of work he has that day. There are four previewing steps that have to do with earning a reward and the reward plan, but these are not preventatively targeting antecedents or anxiety-provoking moments in the day. This plan is mostly reactive.

5. **Are warning signs listed?**

   No.

6. **Is there any consideration of the student's underdeveloped skills? Are they listed in the behavior intervention plan?**

   No.

7. **Is the reinforcement system focused on skill building and skill practice?**

   No it is focused on behavior performance.

8. **Is there a plan to reinforce, practice, and teach these underdeveloped skills?**

   No, this is not addressed.

9. **Are replacement behaviors and strategies taught in this plan?**

   No.

10. **Are there any interaction strategies listed in this plan?**

    No

11. **Does the plan use rewards and consequences based on behavior performance?**

    Yes, it is a reward system based on behavior performance.

12. **Does the plan make any assumptions about the student's ability to behave appropriately and consistently?**

    By reminding him of the rules and rewarding behavior performance, it is assumed Harry will be able to behave well. There is an assumption his misbehavior is due to lack of motivation toward the reward or forgetting the rules.

Case Study: Analyzing Chandra's Behavior Plan

Now review the behavior intervention plan provided in exhibit 4.2 for Chandra, a fourth-grader who can call out and refuse to do work. Then, answer these questions:

1. **Are the target behaviors measurable? Do they represent behaviors that are appropriate and should be increased?**

   No, there are no definitions for the target behaviors. The behaviors are positive and targeted to be increased.

2. **Is there a list of antecedents (collected from data) and corresponding interventions to reduce the student's anxiety in those activities or moments?**

   No.

3. **Is the functional hypothesis based on ABC notes or a functional behavior analysis, and is the hypothesis written on the plan?**

   No.

4. **What percentage of the plan is preventative, and what percentage is reactive?**

   It is vastly reactive. There is one preventative intervention: the student is given a graphic organizer during writing. The rest of the interventions is based on praising appropriate behavior performance and previewing the reward plan.

5. **Are warning signs listed?**

   No.

6. **Is there any consideration of the student's underdeveloped skills? Are they listed in the behavior intervention plan?**

   There is one accommodation for writing, although writing as an underdeveloped skill is not mentioned.

7. **Is the reinforcement system focused on skill building and skill practice?**

   No, it is focused on behavior performance.

8. **Is there a plan to reinforce, practice, and teach these underdeveloped skills?**

   No, there is no plan other than to use a graphic organizer during writing.

9. **Are replacement behaviors and strategies taught in this plan?**

   No.

10. **Are there any interaction strategies listed in this plan?**

    No.

11. **Does the plan use rewards and consequences based on behavior performance?**

    Yes, the plan rewards and has consequences for behavior performance.

12. **Does the plan make any assumptions about the student's ability to behave appropriately and consistently?**

    The assumption is that Chandra can follow the rules with reminders and motivation (i.e., rewards and consequences) only and that it is in her control. There is no mention of antecedents or underdeveloped skills that contribute to her behavior.

CHAPTER 5

Exercise: Practicing Demands

Alone or with your team, restate the direction with each of the demand strategies, and practice aloud, using a neutral tone.

Original direction: **"Can you move over and make room for George?"**

Demand strategy	Restated direction
Avoid yes-or-no questions	"Where are you going to sit to make room for George?"
Choices	"Do you want to sit here or here to make room for George?"
Declarative language	"Oh, I notice George needs a seat . . . hmm."
Indirect	"Linda Sue, thank you for moving over so that George can find room. I bet others will, too."
Deliver, and move	Write a note asking the student to move over, hand it to the student, and walk away quickly.
Extended time to comply	"By the time I finish passing out papers, I need you to move over for George."
Give demands privately	Take the student aside, and whisper the direction.
Nonverbal	Gesture to the student to move over.
Preview the demand	"In one minute, I am going to ask you to move over to make room for George."
Provide rationale first	"Oh dear, I don't want George to have to stand during class. Could you move over?"
Combination	Gesture while complimenting others on moving over.

Original direction: **"Stop calling out, and raise your hand!"**

Demand strategy	Restated direction
Avoid yes-or-no questions	Not applicable, as this is not a yes-or-no issue but a directive.
Choices	"You can raise your hand or write down your answer."
Declarative language	"Oh, I am looking to call on someone with their hand up."
Indirect	"I love calling on students with their hand raised."

Demand strategy	Restated direction
Deliver, and move	Whisper to the student, "Raise your hand," and move away quickly to talk to another student.
Extended time to comply	"I would like to hear that. Please raise your hand and tell us before the end of class."
Give demands privately	Whisper to the student a reminder to raise his hand.
Nonverbal	Teacher puts her finger on her mouth or raises her own hand as a model.
Preview the demand	"It's time for math; I am going to ask you to raise your hand."
Provide rationale first	"Oh dear, I want to call on everyone equally, which is easier when people raise their hand."
Combination	Put finger to mouth, and then move away.

Original direction: "Put the scissors down, please."

Demand strategy	Restated direction
Avoid yes-or-no questions	Not applicable; this is not a yes-or-no question.
Choices	"Where are you going to put those scissors? In the bin or in your desk?"
Declarative language	"I notice the scissors are close to other kids."
Indirect	"Javon, I like how you are keeping your scissors on the desk."
Deliver, and move	Give direction, and then walk across the room to make a phone call to the office.
Extended time to comply	Not applicable; the direction needs to be more immediate.
Give demands privately	Whisper the direction to the student.
Nonverbal	Gesture for the student to put the scissors down.
Preview the demand	Not applicable; the direction needs to be more immediate
Combination	Whisper, "Oh, I don't want anyone to get hurt. Could you please put the scissors down?"

CHAPTER 6

Case Study: Making a FAIR Behavior Intervention Plan for Aton

Student's Name: _____Aton_____   Date: ___5/2_____

TARGETED BEHAVIORS (use measurable definitions only):

Listening to directions: Aton will comply with a direction, as evidenced by his actions within ten seconds of the direction's being given. Example: Aton takes snack wrappers off desk and discards them in the trash when asked. Nonexample: Aton doesn't remove snack wrappers when asked, because he didn't hear the teacher.

Safe behavior: Aton will stay with his teacher and his class, unless he is given permission to leave a designated area, and will safely open and close doors. Example: Aton will gently close the classroom door behind him. Nonexample: Aton doesn't catch the door, and it slams behind him.

WARNING SIGNS (list behavior clues that indicate the student's behavior may be escalating):

Pacing around the room, saying derogatory statements like "this is stupid," laughing loudly

F **Functional Hypothesis**

Document all instances of targeted behaviors, using ABC data sheet (minimum of ten incidents):

Antecedents	*Consequences*
Academic demands	Successfully avoids demands
Writing	Avoids writing
Unstructured times	One-to-one attention from an adult (principal)
Transitions	Negative attention from peers

Setting Events of Note

After weekends with his father, Mondays and Tuesdays are difficult.

What is the Functional Hypothesis Based on ABC Notes (can check more than one)?

☑ Escape   ☑ Attention
☐ Tangible   ☐ Sensory

Accommodations

Environmental

☑ Provide safe space in classroom
☑ Modify schedule
☑ Schedule breaks
☑ Arrange alternative recess
☑ Arrange alternative lunch

☑ Provide other areas of competence: *Reading to a Kindergartener, deliver notices for the teacher*

_____

Executive functioning

☑ Use visual schedules
☑ Use segmented clock during nonpreferred activities

☑ Put organization time in schedule
☑ Present only a few problems or items at a time

Curriculum

☑ Embedded choice
☑ Use of technology: *use tablet or laptop programs for academic instruction/ practice*
☑ Use word processing
☑ Use "How I Feel About Writing" sheet

☑ Offer hands-on, experiential lessons
☑ Give open-ended, flexible assignments
☑ Use student's own interests in curriculum

Replacement behaviors

☑ Teach asking for a break appropriately

☑ Teach asking for help appropriately during demand or otherwise

Underdeveloped skill development

☑ Positive thinking

☑ Self-monitoring

☑ Flexible thinking

☑ Executive functioning

☑ Self-regulation

☑ Social skills

Self-regulation and self-monitoring

☑ Prompt for "body checks" throughout the day

☑ Have the student practice self-calming: *twice per day for five minutes each*

☑ Use visual self-regulation list

☑ Use the FAIR Plan self-monitoring sheet

Breaks

☑ Create data sheet to determine helpful break choices and if breaks are working throughout day

☑ Use biofeedback

☑ Create a break menu/visual list to help the student make helpful break choices

☑ Use cognitive distraction break choices

☑ Schedule breaks—noncontingent escape from demands to minimize frustration: *after non-preferred activities*

☑ Use of technology: *biofeedback during breaks*

Interaction Strategies

- ☑ Work on explicit relationship building
- ☑ Use noncontingent reinforcement
- ☑ Use leadership-building and self-esteem-building activities
- ☑ Use validation
- ☑ Prompt student to avoid asking yes-or-no questions and to ask in a different way

Transitions

- ☑ Support abrupt transitions; use graduated transition strategies:
  warm ups, such as coloring books, are a good way to start class
- ☑ Include transition warnings:
  Say, "Find a stopping place," and use a countdown to let him know when next activity is starting
- ☑ Offer accommodations to support initiating or starting:
  - *Preview: do the first two problems with him in the morning, and then give him that work later, always helping him start the first two problems*
- ☑ Explicit instruction of transitions:
  - *Teach him to ask for help or to let the teacher know he needs help getting started (make a "Help getting started" pass that he can hand to you so that he doesn't have to ask for help in front of peers)*
  - *Teach him how to pick an activity that is appropriate for the time allotted*

Strategies for giving demands

- ☑ Avoid power struggles
- ☑ Embed choice in the demand
- ☑ Give demand, and move away
- ☑ Give extended time for compliance
- ☑ Use humor when appropriate
- ☑ Make it a game
- ☑ Provide the rationale first
- ☑ Switch adults

To reduce negative-attention seeking from a teacher

☑ Have Aton agree to a positive attention system he is comfortable with

Catching Them Early

☑ Respond to any sudden change in behavior with supportive response
☑ Use daily check-in sheet with multiple choice

R Response Strategies

☑ Start with assigning bonus points for the following: *practicing self-calming, asking for help, taking a break when asked or initiating a break, complying with body checks*
☑ Answer simple questions
☑ Avoid ignoring the student
☑ Frustration tolerance: if he exhibits low tolerance for work, start in small increments, and give escape from work (break), and build up workload slowly
☑ Use processing sheet (specify when, in what format, and supported by whom) to teach not to punish

For escape-motivated behavior

☑ Avoid responses that would reinforce escape-motivated behavior, such as time-outs and removal from class

For attention-motivated behavior

☑ Avoid responses such as one-on-one talks or repeatedly telling the student to stop

Bonus points assigned tfor the following strategies/skill practice:

1. _____
2. _____
3. _____
4. _____

DATA COLLECTION

List the target behaviors on which you will collect (or will continue to collect) data, and list which data sheets you will be using:

Teacher will continue to collect ABC data on any unsafe, safe, listening to directions and noncompliant behaviors, as well as taking frequency on all the behaviors at baseline and then after implementation of this plan.

IMPLEMENTATION CHECKLIST

Implementation checklists have been created for the two interventions (breaks and the teaching of self-calming) and for the total plan.

FAIR PLAN COLLABORATION

Please list all involved team members and their roles in implementing the plan:

Staff _Teacher_   Role/responsibility: _Implementing this plan_

Staff _Special education teacher_   Role/responsibility: _Explicit instruction of underdeveloped skills_

Staff _Social worker_   Role/responsibility: _Communicating with family around setting events_

SIGNATURES

_____   _____

Staff signature   Date

_____   _____

Parent/guardian signature   Date

Notes

Introduction

1. Kathleen Ries Merikangas et al., "Lifetime Prevalence of Mental Disorders in U.S. Adolescents: Results from the National Comorbidity Survey Replication—Adolescent Supplement (NCS-A)," *Journal of the American Academy of Child and Adolescent Psychiatry* 49, no. 10 (October 2010): 980–989.

Chapter 1

1. Vincent Mark Durand, *Severe Behavior Problems: A Functional Communication Training Approach* (New York: Guilford Press, 1990), 11–14.

Chapter 2

1. John O. Cooper, Timothy E. Heron, and William L. Heward, *Applied Behavior Analysis* (Upper Saddle River, NJ: Pearson/Merrill-Prentice Hall, 2008).
2. Ibid., 696.
3. Jeffrey H. Tiger, Gregory P. Hanley, and Jennifer Bruzek, "Functional Communication Training: A Review and Practical Guide," *Behavior Analysis in Practice* 1, no. 1 (2008): 16–23.
4. Cooper, Heron, and Heward, *Applied Behavior Analysis*.
5. Sidney W. Bijou, Robert F. Peterson, and Marion H. Ault, "A Method to Integrate Descriptive and Experimental Field Studies at the Level of Data and Empirical Concepts," Journal of Applied Behavior Analysis 1, no. 2 (1968); Beth Sulzer-Azaroff and G. Roy Mayer, Applying Behavior-Analysis Procedures with Children and Youth (New York: Holt, Rinehart and Winston, 1977), 48–77.
6. For setting events, see Cooper, Heron, and Heward, *Applied Behavior Analysis*.

Chapter 3

1. John O. Cooper, Timothy E. Heron, and William L. Heward, *Applied Behavior Analysis* (Upper Saddle River, NJ: Pearson/Merrill-Prentice Hall, 2008).
2. Carol Gray and Stacy Arnold, *The New Social Story Book* (Arlington, TX: Future Horizons 2010). Bottom of Form

3. Allison Lowy Apple, Felix Billingsley, and Ilene S. Schwartz, "Effects of Video Modeling Alone and with Self-Management on Compliment-Giving Behaviors of Children with High-Functioning ASD," *Journal of Positive Behavior Interventions* 7, no. 1 (2005): 33–46.

4. Rachael D. Waller and Thomas S. Higbee, "The Effects of Fixed-Time Escape on Inappropriate and Appropriate Classroom Behavior," *Journal of Applied Behavior Analysis* 43, no. 1 (2010): 149–153.

5. Kate J. Hodson et al., "Can Clark and Wells' (1995) Cognitive Model of Social Phobia Be Applied to Young People?" *Behavioural and Cognitive Psychotherapy* 36, no. 4 (July 2008): 449–461; David M. Clark and Adrian Wells, "A Cognitive Model of Social Phobia," in *Social Phobia: Diagnosis, Assessment, and Treatment*, ed. Richard G. Heimberg et al. (New York: Guilford Press, 1995), 69–93.

6. Robert Brooks, "The Search for Islands of Competence: A Metaphor of Hope and Strength," *Reclaiming Children and Youth* 16, no. 1 (2007): 11–13.

Chapter 4

1. Kathleen Ries Merikangas et al, "Lifetime Prevalence of Mental Disorders in U.S. Adolescents: Results from the National Comorbidity Survey Replication—Adolescent Supplement (NCS-A)," *Journal of the American Academy of Child and Adolescent Psychiatry* 49, no. 10 (October 2010): 980–989.

2. Kenneth W. Merrell, *Helping Students Overcome Depression and Anxiety: A Practical Guide* (New York: Guilford Press, 2008), 7.

3. Amy F. T. Arnsten, "Stress Signalling Pathways That Impair Prefrontal Cortex Structure and Function," *Nature Reviews Neuroscience* 10, no. 6 (2009): 410–422.

4. Florin Dolcos and Gregory McCarthy, "Brain Systems Mediating Cognitive Interference by Emotional Distraction," *Journal of Neuroscience* 26, no. 7 (2006): 2072–2079; Shaozheng Qin et al., "Acute Psychological Stress Reduces Working Memory-Related Activity in the Dorsolateral Prefrontal Cortex," *Biological Psychiatry* 66, no. 1 (2009): 25–32; P. S. Goldman-Rakic, "The Prefrontal Landscape: Implications of Functional Architecture for Understanding Human Mentation and the Central Executive," in *The Prefrontal Cortex: Executive and Cognitive Functions*, ed. A. C. Roberts, T. W. Robbins, and L. Weiskrantz (New York: Oxford University Press, 1998), 87–102.

5. Jerome Schultz, "The Stress Connection: The Missing Piece of the LD Puzzle," paper presented at the annual meeting of the Learning Disabilities Association of America, Chicago, February 12, 2012.

6. For the numbers of students who will experience anxiety, see Merikangas et al., "Lifetime Prevalence of Mental Disorders."

Chapter 5

1. P. S. Goldman-Rakic, "The Prefrontal Landscape: Implications of Functional Architecture for Understanding Human Mentation and the Central Executive," in *The Prefrontal Cortex: Executive and Cognitive Functions*, ed. A. C. Roberts, T. W. Robbins, and L. Weiskrantz (New York: Oxford University Press, 1998), 87–102; Amy F. T. Arnsten, "Stress Signalling Pathways

That Impair Prefrontal Cortex Structure and Function," *Nature Reviews Neuroscience* 10, no. 6 (2009): 410–422.

2. Carol Gray, *Comic Strip Conversations: Illustrated Interactions That Teach Conversation Skills to Students with Autism and Related Disorders* (Arlington, TX: Future Horizons, 1994).

3. Jeannie Golden, "Assessment and Treatment of Emotional and Immoral Behaviors of Children," paper presented at the meeting of the Association for Behavior Analysis International, San Antonio, TX, May 2010.

4. Ibid.

Chapter 7

1. John W. McKenna, Andrea Flower, and Stephen Ciullo, "Measuring Fidelity to Improve Intervention Effectiveness," *Intervention in School and Clinic* (April 30, 2014).

2. This sheet was developed by Dan Almeia (Director of ABA Services, Newton Public Schools) and is used with permission.

3. Alan D. Poling, Laura L. Methot, and Mark G. LeSage, *Fundamentals of Behavior Analytic Research* (New York: Plenum Press, 1995); John O. Cooper, Timothy E. Heron, and William L. Heward, *Applied Behavior Analysis* (Upper Saddle River, NJ: Pearson/Merrill-Prentice Hall, 2008).

4. Frank M. Gresham, "Assessment of Treatment Integrity in School Consultation and Prereferral Intervention," *School Psychology Review* 18, no. 1 (1989): 37–50; Frank M. Gresham et al., "Treatment Integrity in Learning Disabilities Intervention Research: Do We Really Know How Treatments Are Implemented?" *Learning Disabilities Research & Practice (Lawrence Erlbaum)* 15, no. 4 (2000): 198–205; Kathleen L. Lane et al., "Treatment Integrity: An Essential—but Often Forgotten—Component of School-Based Interventions," *Preventing School Failure* 48, no. 3 (2004): 36–43.

5. McKenna, Flower, and Ciullo, "Measuring Fidelity."

6. Lisa M. Hagermoser Sanetti and Thomas R. Kratochwill, "Treatment Integrity in Behavioral Consultation: Measurement, Promotion, and Outcomes," *International Journal of Behavioral Consultation and Therapy* 4, no. 1 (2008): 95–114.

7. Daryl Mellard, "Fidelity of Implementation Within a Response to Intervention (RtI) Framework: Tools for Schools," National Center on Response to Intervention, 2010, www.ped .state.nm.us/rti/dl11/11-Fidelity%20of%20Implementation%20guidev5.pdf.

Appendix B

1. Two national training programs are CPI (Crisis Prevention Institute, www.crisisprevention. com) and Therapeutic Crisis Intervention System (http://rccp.cornell.edu/tcimainpage.html).

2. Part of the safety protocol is adapted with permission from the work of Katherine Terras at the University of North Dakota. Feedback on all protocols was given by Newton Public Schools staff.

3. The PREPaRE School Crisis Prevention and Intervention Training Curriculum (www.nasponline .org/prepare/index.aspx) is one example of a training for school personnel.

Acknowledgments

To the all the students I have been honored to work with, thank you for patiently guiding me to reach new levels of understanding and for teaching me the humility and flexibility to persist in finding solutions. The perseverance and strength you have demonstrated in overcoming challenges has taught me that change is always possible.

To all teachers and school professionals, especially those in the Newton and Cambridge public school systems, thank you for your dedication to supporting hard-to-reach students and for digging deep to sustain your efforts to foster the progress we know they are capable of, even when they make us question ourselves and our abilities.

To Nancy Rappaport, thank you for encouraging me to put my ideas on paper and partnering with me to cowrite *The Behavior Code*. I am grateful for the opportunity, without which this guide would not have been possible.

To Nancy Walser, for your supportive guidance and vision and for imparting your wisdom—I am so grateful. To Sarah Reinfeld for your intelligence, keen feedback, masterful editing, and support of this project.

To Katherine Terras, David Summergrad, Diana Baker, Jeffrey Benson, Jerome Schultz, Dan Almeida, Jill Parkin, Jailyn Correa, Julie Young, Patricia West, and Jessica Everett, thank you for providing feedback, reviewing chapters, and sharing your expertise. To Amity Kulis, Stephanie Monaghan-Blout, Angela Currie, and Kelly Chalin, thank you for helping me find much-needed resources.

Above all, thank you to my parents, for not only for copyediting, but for continuously supporting me and for instilling in me a personal responsibility for others through your example. I dedicate this book to you with all my love and gratitude. And to my family, a collection of people I admire and aspire to resemble, thank you for continuing to shape who I am for the better, particularly my nephews for always reminding me what is important.

About the Author

Jessica Minahan, MEd, BCBA, is a board-certified behavior analyst and special educator. She is Director of Behavioral Services at Neuropsychology & Education Services for Children & Adolescents (NESCA), in Newton, Massachusetts, as well as a behavior consultant to schools nationwide. She also holds an adjunct professor position in the special education department at Boston University.

Jessica has over sixteen years of experience in public school systems supporting students with mental health challenges who exhibit concerning behavior. She has extensive experience supporting students with explosive and unsafe behavior, anxiety, trauma histories, emotional and behavioral disabilities, and high-functioning autism. Jessica specializes in staff training and creating behavior intervention plans and systems that combine a behavioral approach with a deep understanding of the student's psychological profile.

Jessica holds a BS in intensive special education from Boston University and a dual master's degree in special education and elementary education from Wheelock College. She has a certificate of graduate study (CGS) in teaching children with autism from the University of Albany and received her behavior analyst training from Northeastern University. A sought-after international public speaker, Jessica has spoken on subjects ranging from effective interventions for students with anxiety to supporting hard-to-reach students in full-inclusion public school settings. She is a blogger for the *Huffington Post* and the coauthor of *The Behavior Code: A Practical Guide to Understanding and Teaching the Most Challenging Students*, with Nancy Rappaport (Harvard Education Press, 2012). Her speaking schedule, other publications, and more information are available at www.jessicaminahan.com.

Index